T0097075

EARLY HISTORIES
and DESCRIPTIONS
of

ONEIDA COUNTY

NEW YORK

COMPILED and EDITED by
G. MARTIN SLEEMAN

Published by
North Country Books, Inc.
Publisher—Distributor
18 Irving Place
Utica, New York 13501-5618

Early Histories & Descriptions
of
Oneida County, New York

Copyright © 1990
by G. Martin Sleeman

All Rights Reserved
No part of this book may be reproduced
in any manner without written
permission of the publisher.

ISBN 0-932052-83-5

Library of Congress Cataloging-in-Publication Data

Early histories and descriptions of Oneida County, New York/compiled
and edited by G. Martin Sleeman.
　　　p.　　　cm.
　　Includes biographical references and index.
　　ISBN 0-932052-83-5:
　　1. Oneida County (N.Y.)—History.　2. Oneida County (N.Y.)-
-Description and travel.　　I. Sleeman, G. Martin, 1918-
II. Title: Early history and description of Oneida County, New
York.
F127.05E27　　1990
974.7'62—dc20
　　　　　　　　　　　　　　　　　　　　90-7930
　　　　　　　　　　　　　　　　　　　　CIP

Published by
North Country Books, Inc.
Publisher—Distributor
18 Irving Place
Utica, New York 13501-5618

Dedicated to my wife
Diana

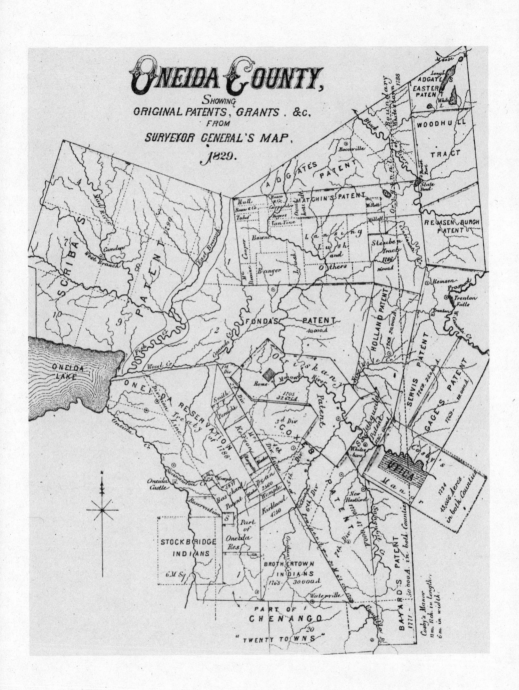

Table of Contents

Illustrations

Maps

Preface

The purpose of this book is to bring together and preserve observations and accounts about Oneida County written prior to the 1851 publication of Pomroy Jones' *Annals and Recollections of Oneida County*. This material, often by travelers just passing through, is in books, or collections of documents, long out of print and difficult to locate. Only a few copies of the lectures of William Tracy and Othniel S. Williams are still in existence and I am grateful to the Oneida County Historical Society for their permission to copy and publish their material. Except for individual incidents and local folklore the history of Oneida County is representative of the development of Upstate New York following the Revolutionary War.

At the time of the arrival of white men into Upstate New York the area was controlled by the Iroquois confederacy - the "longhouse builders." It is believed that originally those tribes came from Canada and settled in the central part of the state. The Mohawks, "people of the place of flint," Onondagas, "on the mountain," and the Senecas, "great hill people." Later two other tribes were formed: the Oneidas, "people of the standing stone," and Cayugas, "where they land boats." Early in the eighteenth century they permitted the Tuscaroras to join them and they were assigned the area below the Onondagas and Oneidas.

The confederacy was formed sometime between 1450-1500 A.D. According to legend it was a man called Hiawatha who traveled between the tribes to persuade them to stop fighting among themselves and form an alliance. Hiawatha is also credited with the invention of wampum. While today we generally think of wampum as a form of currency it also served as a substitute for writing. It was exchanged to signify the agreement between parties, a peace treaty, invitation to council meetings, message of condolence as well as a seal of office.

The Iroquois have been referred to as the "Romans of the New World" because of their governmental organization, equally appropriate would be the title "Spartans." No other group in North America was so dedicated to the training for, and waging, war as the Iroquois. By 1700 A.D. they dominated the area from Canada to the northern southern states and from the Atlantic to the Great Lakes.

Under British rule the eastern portion of Oneida County was in Tryon County, the western part was Indian territory. When New York State became independent the name was changed to Montgomery County and the western boundary extended to take in more of the Indian territory. In 1791 Montgomery was subdivided into Tioga, Otsego and Herkimer Counties. Oneida County was set off from Herkimer on the 15th of March 1798 and at that time contained what is now St. Lawrence, Lewis, Jefferson and Oswego Counties. St. Lawrence was created as a separate county in 1802, Lewis and Jefferson in 1805 and Oswego on the 1st of March 1816.

Originally Oneida County was divided into thirteen townships: Augusta, Bridgewater, Camden, Deerfield, Floyd, Paris, Remsen, Rome, Steuben, Trenton, Western, Westmoreland and Whitestown. Later some of these were subdivided into:

1802 Vernon	1823 Annsville
1802 Verona	1827 New Hartford
1804 Sangerfield fr. Chenango Co.	1827 Kirkland
1805 Florence	1829 Marshall
1805 Boonville fr. Leyden	1832 Marcy
1807 Orange*	1846 Ava
1811 Lee	1869 Forestport
1817 Utica	

While there were a few traders outside of Fort Stanwix prior to the Revolution they fled at the onset of hostilities. When the preliminary peace treaty was signed on the 30th of November 1782

* Name changed to Bengal in 1808 and the current Vienna in 1816.

giving this country its freedom it did not make any provisions to cover those Iroquois tribes that had sided with the British during the war. Therefore, peace did not come to the area until the signing of a peace treaty with them at Fort Stanwix in 1784. The continuous development of the county dates the 5th of June 1784 when Hugh White arrived with his family.

*   *   *

The work of William W. Campbell (1806-1881) appears twice in this book: The "History of the Six Nations" is taken from his *Annals of Tryon County* published in 1831, and "DeWitt Clinton's Journal of 1810" is in his *Life Writings of DeWitt Clinton*. William Campbell was born in Cherry Valley, New York the grandson of Col. Samuel Campbell who had served under General Herkimer at the battle of Oriskany. After graduating from Union College in 1827 he studied law in New York City and was admitted to the bar in 1831. From 1845 to 1847 he was a member of Congress and from 1849 to 1865 a New York State judge.

The manuscript for a *Journey Into Mohawk and Oneida County* was purchased in the Netherlands in 1895 by the Scotch-born General James Grant Wilson, noted writer and editor. It was first believed that it was written by Arendt Van Corlaer but later research revealed it was the journal of Harmen Meyndertsy van den Bogaert who had been a surgeon stationed at Fort Orange (now Albany) by the Dutch West India Company.

Van den Bogaert (Ca 1612-1648) came to the New World in 1630. After his tour of duty at Fort Orange in 1638 he became part owner of a privateer preying on Spanish ships in the West Indies. In 1645 he returned to Fort Orange but two years later had to flee to the Indians he had visited about a decade earlier to escape from prosecution for a crime he had committed. His capture resulted in the burning of an Indian storehouse. The Indians were later compensated for this loss from the proceeds from the van den Bogaert estate. In an attempt to escape from the jail at Fort Orange he drowned when he fell through the ice.

The first English translation of the journal appeared in the *New York Independent* of October 3, 1895. The manuscript was later purchased by Henry E. Huntington and is now in his library located in San Marino, California. A new translation has recently been made by Charles T. Gehring and William A. Starna and published in a well-annotated *A Journal Into Mohawk and*

Oneida Country - 1634-1635, (Syracuse University Press) 1988.

Elkanah Watson (1758-1842) was a man of courage, vision and perseverance. Early in life he made a reputation as a courier: at the age of seventeen he was entrusted to carry powder to the patriot army at Cambridge; at twenty-two he was assigned the dangerous task of conveying $50,000 to South Carolina and in 1779 dispatches to Benjamin Franklin in France. During his five year stay in Europe he traveled extensively and was a keen observer and reporter paying special attention to the canals in Holland and England. When he returned to New York State he was an active advocate of building a canal from Albany to Lake Erie. In 1791 with Jeremiah Van Rensselaer, Gen. Philip van Cortland and Stephen N. Bayard made a survey for a route for such a canal that would lead to the formation of the Western Lock Navigation Company, the forerunner to the Erie Canal.

From 1807 to 1816 he lived in Pittsfield, Massachusetts and was active in the promotion of agriculture being one of the first to own merino sheep. He founded the Berkshire Agricultural Society and is credited with being the first to hold a county fair. In 1816 he returned to Albany and in 1828 retired to Port Kent on Lake Champlain, New York.

While most of the travelers going through Oneida County were coming from the east, one of the exceptions was a French noble-man who came by way of Buffalo and Oswego. Duke de La Rochefoucauld-Liancourt was born in Paris the 11 January 1747 and died there 27 March 1827. He was the son of Duke d'Eslissac and Marie, the second daughter of Duke Louis-Alexandre de La Rochefoucauld. While he traveled and wrote extensively he was particularly noted for his interest in helping the less fortunate. In 1769 he toured England noting many improvements in agricul-ture and manufacturing which he introduced in France upon his return. He founded a school of arts and trades in Liancourt for children from poor military families. In 1788 it had 130 students and received recognition from King Louis XVI and was given the name "School of the Children of the Fatherland." The Duke was one of the first to found a committee of vaccine and opened a community health center for the people in his area. After the fall of the Bastille he was chosen chairman of the National Assemble and supported the concept of the liberty and conscience and of individual liberty.

The history of New York State would have many blank pages were it not for the prodigious efforts of Edmund Bailey O'Callaghan, M.D. (1797-1880). Dr. O'Callaghan was born in Ireland and educated in Dublin, Paris and Quebec where he was admitted to the practice of medicine in 1832. In 1837 he moved to Albany where he continued to practice medicine and wrote several historical articles published in *The Northern Light*. Mastering the Dutch language in 1848 he published a two-volume *History of the New Netherlands*. For the next twenty-two years he devoted his life to recording and editing documents pertaining to New York State, many of which have since been lost, as well as New York City. In 1851 he published *The Documentary History of the State of New York*, a four-volume work from which Rev. Taylor's Journal was obtained, and in 1861 published *Documents relative to the Colonial History of the State of New York*.

Early reports about Oneida County were written by travelers just passing through using the Mohawk River and Wood Creek. The exception was the Rev. John Taylor, a missionary who spent nearly a month in the county and his report includes towns besides those on the Mohawk River.

Rev. John Taylor (1762-1840) was born in Westfield, Massachusetts. After graduating from Yale in 1784 he became a missionary for the Congregational Church. His health was adversely affected by his arduous travel, so he took up farming in Enfield, Connecticut where he was elected to the state legislature and for several terms served as its speaker. In 1823 he returned to the ministry serving at Henrietta, Monroe County, New York before moving on to Bruce, Macomb County, Michigan.

The first sportsman to report on this area was Christian Schultz, Jr. Very little is known about Mr. Schultz other than he was born in the early 1770s in New York City and died there in 1812 or 1814.

Following the Louisiana Purchase of 1803 there were several visitors to the newly acquired territory but their reports were often inaccurate and written by foreigners who had their personal prejudices about America. Mr. Schultz' description of his trip from New York to New Orleans was one of the first to give an accurate description of the area he traveled and present it from an American's point of view.

New York State has produced many outstanding political leaders and certainly one of the most distinguished was DeWitt Clinton (1769-1828). He was the son of James Clinton, who, with General Sullivan, defeated the Iroquois that had sided with the English during the Revolution. He was also the nephew of George

Clinton, the first governor of New York after it achieved its freedom from England.

DeWitt Clinton attended Columbia College (formerly Kings College) and graduated at the head of his class in 1786. After studying law in New York City he served from 1789 to 1795 as private secretary to his uncle, Governor George Clinton. He was elected to almost every important political office: the New York State Assembly and Senate, United States Senator, Mayor of New York City (1803-1815), New York Lieutenant Governor and Governor. The only position that eluded him was that of the Presidency of the United States, a position he ran for in 1812.

In 1810 he served as a member of a commission to establish a route for a canal to connect the Great Lakes and the Hudson River - his description of traveling through Oneida County is included in this book. After becoming Governor he was instrumental in achieving the construction of this waterway, considered one of the most remarkable engineering feats of the first part of the nineteenth century. Appropriately the sobriquet for the Erie Canal was "Clinton's Ditch."

*   *   *

I am indebted to the Rome Historical Society for their assistance and for supplying most of the illustrations in this book and the help of their researcher Thomas J. Kernan and curator Catherine (Cathy) E. Baty. I wish to thank the Clinton Public and Hamilton College libraries for their cooperation. This book would not have been possible without the aid of Rome's Jervis Library and I am grateful to its assistant director Keith D. Kenna and the very professional and cooperative staff at the reference desk.

G. Martin Sleeman
Rome, New York
1989

ANNALS

OF

TRYON COUNTY;

OR, THE

BORDER WARFARE OF NEW-YORK,

DURING THE REVOLUTION.

BY WILLIAM W. CAMPBELL.

" The whole confederacy, except a little more than half of the Oneidas, took up arms
against us. They hung like the scythe of death upon the rear of our settlements, and
their deeds are inscribed with the scalping-knife and the tomahawk, in characters of
blood, on the fields of Wyoming and Cherry-Valley, and on the banks of the Mohawk."
De Witt Clinton.

NEW-YORK:
PRINTED AND PUBLISHED BY J. & J. HARPER,
NO. 82 CLIFF-STREET.
AND SOLD BY THE PRINCIPAL BOOKSELLERS THROUGHOUT
THE UNITED STATES.

1831.

PROLOQUE

Excerpts from William W. Campbell's
Annals of Tryon County
J. & J. Harper, NY 1831

History of the Six Nations, from the time of the
first settlement of New York to the Commencement
of the Revolution

New York, at the time of its discovery and settlement by the Europeans, was inhabited by a race of men distinquished, above all the other aborigines of this Continent, for their intelligence and prowess. Five distinct and independent tribes, speaking a language radically the same, and practicing similar customs, had united in forming a confederacy which, for durability and power, was unequalled in Indian history. They were the Mohawks, Oneidas, Onondagas, Cayugas, and Senecas, called the Iroquois by the French, and the Five Nations by the English. In cases of great emergency, each tribe or nation acted separately and independently; but a general council usually assembled at Onondaga, near the centre of their territory, and determined upon peace or war, and all other matters which regarded the interests of the whole. The powers of this council appear to have been not much dissimilar to those of the United States Congress under the old confederation.

Their language, though guttural, was sonorous. Their orators studied euphony in their words and in their arrangement. Their graceful attitudes and gestures, and their flowing sentences, rendered their discourses, if not always eloquent, at least highly impressive. An erect and commanding figure, with a blanket thrown loosely over the shoulder, with his naked arm raised, and addressing in impassioned strains a group of similar persons sitting upon the ground around him, would, to use the illustration of an early historian of this State, give no faint picture of Rome in

3

her early days.

They were very methodical in their harangues. When in conference with other nations, at the conclusion of every important sentence of the opposite speaker, a sachem gave a small stick to the orator who was to reply, charging him at the same time to remember it. After a short consultation with the others, he was enabled to repeat most of the discourse, which he answered article by article.

These nations were distinguished for their prowess in war, as well as for their sagacity and eloquence in council. War was their delight. Believing it to be the most honourable employment of men, they infused into their children in early life high ideas of military glory.

They carried their arms into Canada, across the Connecticut, to the banks of the Mississippi, and almost to the Gulf of Mexico. Formidable by their numbers and their skill, they excited respect and awe in the most powerful tribes, and exacted tribute and obedience from the weak. In 1608, the first efficient settlement was made in Canada by Governor Champlain, who founded Quebec. At this time the Five Nations were waging a desperate war with the Hurons and Algonquins, who inhabited a part of that province. Champlain, unfortunately for the colony, entered into an alliance with the latter tribes, and by funishing them with men and firearms, enabled them to gain a temporary ascendance. The confederates, who had always been victorious, and who considered the Hurons and Algonquins as little better than vassals, could not brook this defeat. They applied to, and courted the friendship of the Dutch, who found their way up the Hudson river, and established themselves at Albany, soon after the settlement of Quebec. From them they obtained arms and munitions, and soon regained the influence and power which they had lost. This opportune arrival and assistance of the Dutch, together with their mild, conciliatory manners, endeared them to the Five Nations, who afterward looked up to them for advice and directions in their own affairs, and protected and fought for them with cheerfulness and promptitude. But the interference of the French aroused the indignation of these haughty warriors; for almost a century they harrassed their infant colonies, and visited with a dreadful vengeance both the authors of their disgrace and their descendants. This, if not the iron, was the golden age of the Iroquois. During this period, the hardy German [Dutchman] passed up the Mohawk in his light canoe (sic), and penetrated into the remote bounds of their territory, where he exchanged his merchandise and munitions of war for the peltry of the Indians.

In 1661, the province of New York was surrendered to the English by Peter Stuyvesant, the last of the Dutch governors. The English, perceiving the importance of being on friendly terms with the Indians, exerted themselves to preserve that good understanding which had existed between the latter and the Dutch. Conventions were frequently called at Albany, at which the governors met and conferred with them; presents were distributed liberally, and no opportunity was neglected to impress them with ideas of the wealth and power of the English monarch. The French were not idle. Jealous of the growing power and influence of the English colonies, and desirous of monopolizing the Indian trade, they adopted various plans to detach the Iroquois from their alliance with the English. They endeavoured to break up the confederacy, that they might conquer the nations in detail. They attacked the English, in hopes that, by gaining some splendid victories over them, they would convince the Indians of the weakness of their allies, and of the strength of their enemies. They sent missionaries among them, more desirous of making allies for France than converts to Christianity: in this they partially succeeded; and in 1671, persuaded the Caughnawagas to remove from their settlements on the Mohawk, and to establish themselves in Canada.

In 1688, the vengeance of the Five Nations was again aroused by a stratagem of the Dinondadies, a tribe at war with them, and in alliance with France. The Dinondadies killed several of their ambassadors while going to hold a conference in Canada, and falsely pretended that they had been informed of their journey by the French governor. Incensed at what they considered a great breach of faith, about twelve hundred warriors of the Five Nations landed at Montreal on the 26th July, 1688, and killed about a thousand French-men, women, and children, and carried away twenty-six prisoners, whom they afterward burned alive. The French retaliated for these aggressions by making incursions into the Indian country, and burning their villages.

In 1690, the French made an attack upon Schenectady; took the place by surprise, as it was in the dead of winter, and no danger was apprehended; the whole village was destroyed; about sixty of the inhabitants were killed, and most of the remainder perished, as they fled naked through the snow toward Albany.

This was the first information the colony of New York received that a war was meditated on the part of the French; it was the more perfidious, as negotiations were then pending in Europe for the purpose of settling the claims of the two governments in America. During this war the confederates remained attached to the English, and rendered important services by harassing the frontiers of their enemies. About 1701, a general treaty of peace was made between the French and Five Nations, which put an end to these long and afflicting wars, in which both parties had been sufferers. About 1712, the Monecons, or Tuscaroras, a tribe of Indians living in the Carolinas, made war upon the inhabitants of those colonies; they were vanquished by the colonists, and forced to abondon their country; they are thought to have been allies of the Five Nations in some of their southern expeditions. From a similarity in their language, the Confederates supposed them derived from a common origin; they received them into the confederacy, assigned them a section of their territory to dwell in; after this they were called the Six Nations. The Tuscaroras never possessed the energy and courage of the other confederates. Tradition says that they were obliged to wear a woman's pocket for a tobacco pouch, as a mark of their effeminacy and want of courage.

During the first half of the 18th century, the French missionaries and agents were very successful. That body of men, the French Jesuits, who by their zeal, put to shame many men engaged in a better cause, entered upon this field of labour with great ardour. At one time they doffed the clerical habit, and putting on the Indian garb, accompanied the warriors on distant and hazardous expeditions; and at another, they astonished their savage audience with the splendid and imposing rites and ceremonies of the Romish church. They spoke in glowing terms of the resources and magnificence of le grand Monarque, as they termed the King of France.

They obtained permission for the French to build forts in their territory; and in short, when the last French war broke out in 1754, the four western tribes went over to the French, and took up the hatchet against the English. This war terminated by the complete subjection of Canada, and the annexing it to the British dominions. The Indians, however, witnessing the defeat of the French, many of them returned, before the close of the war, to the English, by whom they were again received as allies.

Major General William Johnson rendered very important services during this war; his complete victory over Baron Dieskau, Sept. 1757, at the head of Lake George, and the capture of Fort

Niagara by him, had aided materially in bringing the war to a successful termination. He was created a Baronet, and Parliament voted him five thousand pounds sterling; he was also appointed general superintendent of Indian affairs; he had settled upon the Mohawk in 1734, having emigrated there from Ireland, and thus rose to rank and affluence. Stern, determined in purpose, at times even arbitrary, sagacious and penetrating, but, when necessary, urbane and conciliatory in his manners, he was eminently qualified for the station to which he was appointed. No person has ever exerted an equal influence over those unlettered children of the forest. He lived at Johnstown, where he had a beautiful residence, and was surrounded by the Mohawks. The Indians looked up to him as their father, paying the utmost deference to his advice, and consulting him on all occasions. Out of compliment to them, he frequently wore in winter their dress; he received them cordially at his house, where sometimes hundreds of them assembled. So great was the respect they had for him, that though the house contained many valuables, nothing was purloined from it, even in their carousals. Being a widower, he received into his family an Indian maiden, a sister of the celebrated sachem Joseph Tayadanaga, called the Brant.

The influence of Sir William continued until his death, about the commencement of the Revolutionary War.

AMERICAN HISTORICAL ASSOCIATION.

ARENT VAN CURLER AND HIS JOURNAL OF 1634-35.

BY

GEN. JAS. GRANT WILSON, D. C. L.,
OF NEW YORK CITY.

(From the Annual Report of the American Historical Association for 1895, pages 81–101.)

WASHINGTON:
GOVERNMENT PRINTING OFFICE.
1896.

SKETCH OF VAN DEN BOGAERT MAP

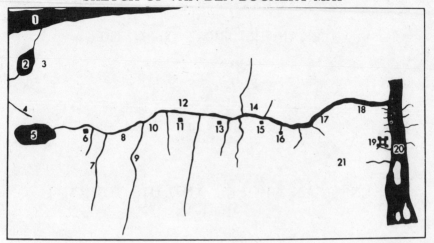

Prepared by the Rome Historical Society

1 River of the French (Rivier Der Fransen)

2 A Lake (Een Meer)

3 Here a marshland with a multitude of beavers (Hier Een Broecklandt Met Swindigh Bevers)

4 River along which the French come (Rivier Waer de Fransen Langhs Comen)

5 Lake of the Oneidas (Meer Der Sinnekens)

6 Oneidas' castle (Onneyuttehage Sinnekens Castiel-66 Huysen)

7 The kill flows to the Delaware (Deese Kill Gaet Naw De Suiyd Rivier)

8 Oneidas' Country (Tsinnikenslandt)

9 A kill that flows to Minckwas land (Een Kil Dat Loop Nae Minckwa-landt)

10 Country of the Mohawks (Tmaehckwaeslandt)

11 Teghnotoga

12 To the north from here about 90 miles to the French (Noordwaerts Hier Van Ongeveer 90 Meylen Naer De Fransen)

13 32 Houses, Schanadissa (32 Huyson, Schanadissa)

14 Much flat land here (Hier Veel Plattelandt)

15 1st castle, Oyhneecagonter 34 houses (Teerste Castiel, Oyhneecagonter 34 Huysen)

16 Eychen der aeckero, Also a castle (Eycken Der Aeckero Oock Een Castiel)

17 By the River (ohyoge)

18 River of the Mohawks (River Der Maehckwaes)

19 Ft. Orange (The Fort)

20 The Hudson (Noord Rivier)

21 At the 1st castle one finds many islands in the river and also much flat land. (By Het Eerste Castiel Vindt Men Veel Eylanden In De Rivier Oock Veel Plattelandt)

Arent Van Curler and
His Journal of 1634-35
(actually journal of Hermen van den Bogaert)

The first European to visit Oneida County, that left a written record, was a Dutch surgeon Hermen van den Bogaert. He left Fort Orange (now Albany) on December 11, 1634 with Jeronimies de Lacroix and Willem Tomassen for a journey up the Mohawk River valley. The purpose was to establish trade with the Indians and to counter the ever growing French influence in Central New York. The trip took them through the middle of Oneida County and into Madison County near Munnsville before returning to Fort Orange.

December 25, 1634 - being Christmas. We rose early in the morning and wanted to go to the Sinnekens [Oneidas]; but, as it was snowing steadily, we could not go, because nobody wanted to go with us to carry our goods. I asked them how many chiefs there were in all, and they told me thirty.

December 26 - In the morning I was offered two pieces of bear's bacon to take with us on the march; and we took our departure, escorted by many of them that walked before and after us. They kept up shouting: *"Allesa roundade!"* that is, to fire pistols; but we did not want to do so, and at last they went back. This day we passed over many a stretch of flat land, and crossed a kill where the water was knee-deep; and I think we kept this day mostly the direction west and northwest. The woods that we traversed consisted in the beginning mostly of oaks, but after three or four hours' marching it was mostly birch trees. It snowed the whole day, so it was very heavy marching over the hills; and after seven leagues [about 16 miles][1], by guess, we arrived at a little house made of bark in the forest, where we lighted a fire and stopped for the night to sleep. It went on snowing, with a sharp, northerly

---

[1]Gilbert W. Hagerty estimated the Dutch league to be about 2⅓ miles. Page 41 *Wampum, War and Trade Goods West of the Hudson*, Heart of Lake Publishing, 1985.

wind. It was very cold.

December 27. Early in the morning again on our difficult march, while the snow lay 2½ feet in some places. We went over hills and through underwood. We saw traces of two bears, and elks, but no savages. There are beech trees; and after marching another seven or eight leagues, at sunset we found another little cabin in the forest, with hardly any bark, but covered with the branches of trees. We made a big fire and cooked our dinner. It was so very cold during this night that I did not sleep more than two hours in all.

December 28. We went as before, and after marching one or two leagues we arrived at a kill that, as the savages told me, ran into the land of the Minquaass, and after another mile we met another kill that runs into the South River, as the savages told me, and here a good many otter and beaver are caught. This day we went over many high hills. The wood was full of great trees, mostly birches; and after seven or eight leagues' marching we did the same as mentioned above. It was very cold.

December 29. We went again, proceeding on our voyage; and after marching a while we came on a very high hill, and as we nearly had mounted it I fell down so hard that I thought I had broken my ribs, but it was only the handle of my cutlass that was broken. We went through a good deal of flat land, with many oaks and handles for axes, and after another seven leagues we found another hut, where we rested ourselves. We made a fire and ate all the food we had, because the savages told us that we were still about four leagues distant from the castle. The sun was near setting as still another of the savages went on to the castle to tell them we were coming. We would have gone with him, but because we felt so very hungry the savages would not take us along with them. The course northwest.

December 30. Without anything to eat we went to the Sinnekens' [Oneida's] castle, and after marching awhile the savages showed me the branch of the river that passes by Fort Orange and past the land of the Maquas. A woman came to meet us, bringing us baked pumpkins to eat. This road was mostly full of birches and beautiful flat land for sowing. Before we reached the castle we saw three graves, just like our graves in length and height; usually their graves are round. These graves were surrounded with palisades that they had split from trees, and they were closed up so nicely that it was a wonder to see. They were painted with

red and white and black paint; but the chief's grave had an
entrance, and at the top of that was a big wooden bird, and all
around were painted dogs, and deer, and snakes, and other
beasts. After four or five leagues' marching the savages still
prayed us to fire our guns, and so we did, but loaded them again
directly and went on to the castle. And we saw to the northwest of
us, a large river [Oneida Lake], and on the other side thereof
tremendously high land that seemed to lie in the clouds. Upon
inquiring closely into this, the savages told me that in this river
the Frenchmen came to trade. And then we marched confidently
to the castle, where the savages divided into two rows, and so let
us pass through them by the gate, which was - the one we went
through - 3½ feet wide, and at the top were standing three big
wooden images, carved like men, and with them I saw three
scalps fluttering in the wind, that they had taken from their foes
as a token of the truth of their victory. This castle has two gates,
one on the east and one on the west side. On the east side a scalp
was also hanging; but this gate was 1½ feet smaller than the
other one. When at last we arrived in the chief's house, I saw
there a good many people that I knew; and we were requested to
sit down in the chief's place where he was accustomed to sit,
because at the time he was not at home, and we felt cold and were
wet and tired. They at once gave us to eat, and they made a good
fire. This castle likewise is situated on a very high hill, and was
surrounded with two rows of palisades. It was 767 paces in cir-
cumference. There are 66 houses, but much better, higher, and
more finished than all the others we saw. A good many houses
had wooden fronts that are painted with all sorts of beasts. There
they sleep mostly on elevated boards, more than any other
savages. In the afternoon one of the council came to me, asking
the reason of our coming into his land, and what we brought for
him as a present. I told him that we did not bring any present,
but that we only paid him a visit. He told us that we were not
worth anything, because we did not bring him a present. Then he
told us how the Frenchmen had come thither to trade with six
men, and had given them good gifts, because they had been
trading in this river with six men in the month of August of this
year. We saw very good axes to cut the underwood, and French
shirts and coats and razors; and this member of the council said
we were scoundrels, and were not worth anything because we
paid not enough for their beaver skins. They told us that the
Frenchmen gave six hands of seawan [wampum] for one beaver,

and all sorts of things more. The savages were pressing closely upon us, so that there was hardly room for us to sit. If they had desired to molest us, we could hardly have been able to defend ourselves; but there was no danger. In this river here spoken of, often six, seven, or eight hundred salmon are caught in a single day. I saw houses where 60, 70, and more dried salmon were hanging.

December 31.   On Sunday the chief of this castle came back (his name is Arenias), and one more man. They told us that they returned from the French savages, and some of the savages shouted *"Jawe Arenias!"* which meant that they thanked him for having come back. And I told him that in the night we should fire three shots; and he said it was all right; and they seemed very well contented. We questioned them concerning the situation [of the places] in their castle and their names, and how far they were away from each other. They showed us with stones and maize grains, and Jeronimus then made a chart of it. And we counted all in leagues how far each place was away from the next. The savages told us that on the high land which we had seen by that lake there lived men with horns on their heads; and they told us that a good many beavers were caught there, too, but they dared not go so far because of the French savages; therefore they thought best to make peace. We fired three shots in the night in honor of the year of our Lord and Redeemer, Jesus Christ.

Praise the Lord above all! In the castle Onneyuttehage, or Sinnekens [Oneida Castle], January 1, 1635.

January 1, 1635.   Another savage scolded at us. We were scoundrels, as told before; and he looked angry. Willem Tomassen got so excited that the tears were running along his cheeks, and the savages, seeing that we were not at all contented, asked us what was the matter, and why we looked so disgusted at him. There were in all 46 persons seated near us; if they had intended to do mischief, they could easily have caught us with their hands and killed us without much trouble; when I had listened long enough to the Indian's chatter I told him that he was a scoundrel himself and he began to laugh, said he was not angry and said: "You must not grow so furious, for we are very glad that you came here." And after that Jeronimus gave the chief two knives, two pairs of scissors, and a few awls and needles that we had with us. And in the evening the savages suspended a band of seawan, and some other stringed seawan that the chief had brought with him from the French savages as a sign of peace and that the French savages were to come in confidence to them.

January 2.   The savages came to us and told us that we had better stop another four or five days. They would provide for all our needs and have us treated nicely; but I told them we could not wait so long as that. They replied that they had sent a message to the Onondagas - that is, the castle next to theirs - but I told them they nearly starved us. Then they said that in future they would look better after us, and twice during this day we were invited to be their guests, and treated to salmon and bear's bacon.

January 3.   Some old men came to us and told us they wanted to be our friends, and they said we need not be afraid. And I replied we were not afraid, and in the afternoon the council sat here - in all, 24 men - and after consulting for a while an old man approached me and laid his hand upon my heart to feel it beat; and then he shouted we really were not afraid at all. After that six more members of the council came, and after that they presented me a coat made of beaver skin, and told me they gave it to me because I came here and ought to be very tired, and he pointed to his and my legs; and besides, it is because you have been marching through the snow. And when I took the coat they shouted three times: *"Netho, netho, netho!"* which means, "This is very well." And directly after that they laid five pieces of beaver skins on my feet, at the same time requesting me that in the future they should receive four hands of seawan and four handbreadths of cloth for every big beaver skin, because we have to go so far with our skins; and very often when we come to your places we do not find any cloth or seawan or axes or kettles, or not enough for all of us, and then we have had much trouble for nothing, and have to go back over a great distance, carrying our goods back again. After we sat for a considerable time, an old man came to us, and translated it to us in the other language, and told us that we did not answer yet whether they were to have four hands of seawan or not for their skins. I told him that we had not the power to promise that, but that we should report about it to the chief at the Manhatans, who was our commander, and that I would give him a definite answer in the spring, and come myself to their land. Then they said to me *"Welsmachkoo,"* you must not lie, and surely come to us in the spring, and report to us about all. And if you will give us four hands of seawan we will not sell our skins to anyone but you; and after that they gave me the five beaver skins, and shouted as hard as they could: *"Netho, netho, netho!"* And then, that everything should be firmly binding, they called or sang *"Ha assironi atsimach koo kent oya kayuig wee Onneyatte Onaondaga Koyocke hoo hanoto wany agweganne hoo schene ha caton scahten franosoni yndicho."* That means that I could go in all these places - they said the names of all the castles - freely and everywhere. I should be provided with a house and a fire and wood and everything I needed; and if I wanted to go to the Frenchmen they would guide me there and back; and after that they shouted again: *"Netho, netho, netho!"* and they made a present of another beaver skin to me, and we ate today bear meat that we were invited to. In this house, belonging to the chief, there were three or four meals a day, and they did not cook in it, as everything was brought in from the other houses in large kettles; for it was the council that took their meals here every day. And whoever then happens to be in the house receives a bowlful of food; for it is the rule here that everyone that comes here has his bowl filled; and if they are short of bowls they bring them and their spoons with them. They go thus and seat themselves side by side; the bowls are then fetched and brought back filled, for a guest that is invited does not rise before he has eaten. Sometimes they sing, and sometimes they do not, thanking the host before they return home.

January 4. Two savages came, inviting us to come and see how they used to drive away the devil. I told them that I had seen it before; but they did not move off, and I had to go; and because I did not choose to go alone I took Jeronimus along. I saw a dozen men together who were going to drive him off. After we arrived the floor of the house was thickly covered with the bark of trees for the hunters of the devil to walk upon. They were mostly old men, and they had their faces all painted with red paint - which they always do when they are going to do anything unusual. Three men among them had a wreath on their heads, on which stuck five white crosses. These wreaths are made of deer hair that they had braided with the roots of a sort of green herb. In the middle of the house they then put a man who was very sick, and who was treated without success during a considerable time. Close by sat an old woman with a turtle shell in her hands. In the turtle shell were a good many beads. She kept clinking all the while, and all of them sang to the measure; then they would proceed to catch the devil and trample him to death; they trampled the bark to atoms so that none of it remained whole, and wher-

Rome Historical Society

*van den Bogaert meeting with the Indians, drawn by
Howard C. Rohmer.*

ever they saw but a little cloud of dust upon the maize, they beat at it in great amazement and then they blew that dust at one another and were so afraid that they ran as if they really saw the devil; and after long stamping and running one of them went to the sick man and took away an otter that he had in his hands; and he sucked the sick man for awhile in his neck and on the back, and after that he spat in the otter's mouth and threw it down; at the same time he ran off like mad through fear. Other men then went to the otter, and then there took place such foolery that it was quite a wonder to see. Yes; they commenced to throw fire and eat fire, and kept scattering hot ashes and red-hot coal in such a way that I ran out of the house. Today another beaver skin was presented to me.

January 5.   I bought four dried salmon and two pieces of bear bacon that was about nine inches thick; and we saw thicker, even. They gave us beans cooked with bear bacon to eat today, and further nothing particular happened.

January 6.   Nothing particular than that I was shown a parcel of flint stones wherewith they make fire when they are in the forest. Those stones would do very well for firelock guns.

January 7.   We received a letter from Marten Gerritsen, dated from the last of December; it was brought by a Sinneken [Oneidian] that arrived from our fort. He told us that our people grew very uneasy about our not coming home, and that they thought we had been killed. We ate fresh salmon only two days caught, and we were robbed today of six and a half hands of seawan that we never saw again.

January 8.   Arenias came to me to say that he wanted to go with me to the fort and take all his skins to trade. Jeronimus tried to sell his coat here, but he could not get rid of it.

January 9.   During the evening the Onondagas came. There were six old men and four women. They were very tired from the march, and brought with them some bear skins. I came to meet them, and thanked them that they came to visit us; and they welcomed me, and because it was very late I went home.

January 10.   Jeronimus burned the greater part of his pantaloons, that dropped in the fire during the night, and the chief's mother gave him cloth to repair it, and Willem Tomassen repaired it.

January 11.   At ten o'clock in the morning the savages came to me and invited me to come to the house where the Onondagans sat in council. "They will give you presents"; and I went there with Jeronimus; took our pistols with us and sat alongside of them, near an old man of the name of Canastogeera, about 55 years of age; and he said: "Friends, I have come here to see you and to talk to you;" wherefore we thanked him, and after they had sat in council for a long time an interpreter came to me and gave me five pieces of beaver skin because we had come into their council. I took the beaver skins and thanked them, and they shouted three times *"Netho!"* And after that another five beaver skins that they laid upon my feet, and they gave them to me because I had come into their council-house. We should have been given a good many skins as presents if we had come into his land; and they earnestly requested me to visit their land in the summer, and after that gave me another four beaver skins and asked at the same time to be better paid for their skins. They would bring us a great quantity if we did; and if I came back in the summer to their land we should have three or four savages along with us to look all around that lake and show us where the Frenchmen came trading with their shallops [sloop]. And when we gathered our fourteen beavers they again shouted as hard as they could, *"Zinae netho!"* and we fired away with our pistols and gave the chief two pairs of knives, some awls, and needles; and then we were informed we might take our departure. We had at the time five pieces of salmon and two pieces of bear bacon that we were to take on the march, and here they gave a good many loaves and even flour to take with us.

January 12. We took our departure; and when we thought everything was ready the savages did not want to carry our goods - twenty-eight beaver skins, five salmon, and some loaves of bread - because they all had already quite enough to carry; but after a good deal of grumbling and nice words they at last consented and carried our goods. Many savages walked along with us and they shouted, *"Alle sarondade!"* that is, to fire the pistols; and when we came near the chief's grave we fired three shots, and they went back. It was about nine o'clock when we left this place and walked only about five leagues through 2½ feet of snow. It was a very difficult road, so that some of the savages had to stop in the forest and sleep in the snow. We went on, however, and reached a little cabin, where we slept.

January 13. Early in the morning we were on our journey

again, and after going seven or eight leagues we arrived at another hut, where we rested awhile, cooked our dinner, and slept. Arenias pointed out to me a place on a high mountain, and said that after ten days' marching we could reach a big river there where plenty of people are living, and where plenty of cows and horses are; but we had to cross the river for a whole day and then to proceed for six days more in order to reach it. This was the place which we passed on the 29th of December. He did us a great deal of good.

January 14. On Sunday we made ready to proceed, but the chief wished to go bear hunting and wanted to stop here but, because it was fine weather, I went alone with two or three savages. Here two Maquas Indians joined us, as they wanted to go and trade elk skins.

January 15. In the morning, two hours before daylight, after taking breakfast with the savages, I proceeded on the voyage, and when it was nearly dark again the savages made a fire in the wood, as they did not want to go farther, and I came about three hours after dark to a hut where I had slept on the 26th of December. It was very cold. I could not make a fire, and was obliged to walk the whole night to keep warm.

January 16. In the morning, three hours before dawn, as the moon rose, I searched for the path, which I found at last; and because I marched so quickly I arrived about nine o'clock on very extensive flat land. After having passed over a high hill I came to a very even footpath that had been made through the snow by the savages who had passed this way with much venison, because they had come home to their castle after hunting; and about ten o'clock I saw the castle and arrived there about twelve o'clock. Upward of one hundred people came out to welcome me, and showed me a house where I could go. They gave me a white hare to eat that they caught two days ago. They cooked it with walnuts, and they gave me a piece of wheaten bread a savage, that had arrived here from Fort Orange on the fifteenth of this month, had brought with him. In the evening more than forty fathoms of seawan were divided among them as the last will of the savages that died of the smallpox. It was divided in the presence of the chief and the nearest friends. It is their custom to divide among the chief and nearest friends. And in the evening the savages gave me two bear skins to cover me, and they brought rushes to lay under my head, and they told us that our kinsmen wanted us very much to come back.

January 17. Jeronimus and Tomassen, with some savages, joined us in this castle, Tenotagehage, and they still were all right; and in the evening I saw another hundred fathoms of sea-wan divided among the chief and the friends of the nearest blood.

January 18. We went again to this castle. In some of the houses we saw more than forty or fifty deer cut in quarters and dried; but they gave us very little of it to eat. After marching half a league we passed through the village of Kawaoge, and after another half league we came to the village of Osquage. The chief, Ohquahoo, received us well, and we waited here for the chief, Arenias, whom we had left in the castle Te Notooge.

January 19. We went as fast as we could in the morning, proceeding on the march; and after going half a league we arrived at the third castle, named Schanadisse, and I looked around in some of the houses to see whether there were any skins. I met nine Onondagas there with skins, who I told to go with me to the second castle, where the chief, Taturot, I should say Tonewerot, was at home, who welcomed us at once, and gave us a very fat piece of venison, which we cooked; and when we were sitting at dinner we received a letter from Marten Gerritsen, brought us by a savage that came in search of us, and was dated January 18. We resolved to proceed at once to the first castle, and to depart on the morrow for Fort Orange, and a good three hours before sunset we arrived at the first castle. We had bread baked for us again, and packed the three beavers we had received from the chief when we had first come here. We slept here this night and ate here.

January 20. In the morning, before daylight, Jeronimus sold his coat for four beaver skins to an old man. We set forth at one hour before daylight, and after marching by guess two leagues the savages pointed to a high mountain where their castle stood nine years before. They had been driven out by the Mahicans, and after that time they did not want to live there. After marching seven or eight leagues we found that the hunters' cabins had been burned, so we were obliged to sleep under the blue sky.

January 21. We proceeded early in the morning, and after a long march we took a wrong path that was the most walked upon; but as the savages knew the paths better than we did they returned with us, and after eleven leagues' marching we arrived, the Lord be praised and thanked, at Fort Orange, January 21, anno 1635.

MEN AND TIMES

OF

THE REVOLUTION;

OR,

MEMOIRS OF ELKANAH WATSON,

INCLUDING

Journals of Travels in Europe and America,

FROM 1777 TO 1842,

WITH

HIS CORRESPONDENCE WITH PUBLIC MEN, AND REMINISCENCES
AND INCIDENTS OF THE REVOLUTION,

EDITED BY HIS SON,

WINSLOW C. WATSON.

New-York:
DANA AND COMPANY, PUBLISHERS,
No. 381 Broadway.

1856.

Journal of Elkanah Watson

Elkanah Watson (1758-1842) was a very successful business man having organized the Bank of Albany (NY). He was active in serving the interest of the newly formed republic. In 1779 he carried money and dispatches to Benjamin Franklin in France. While in Europe he studied the waterway system in Holland and upon his return to New York promoted the development of canals in the state. Among his other interests was the encouragement of agriculture and in 1810 staged a "cattle show" in Pittsfield, Massachusetts and today is considered to be the "father" of county fairs.

The territory known as the German flats had been long inhabited, and was densely occupied by a German population. This people had suffered severely during the war of Independence, from the ravages of the Tories and Indians, and had been nearly extirpated. Impressive vestiges of these events were exhibited throughout the entire district. Their safety was only secured by the erection of numerous block-houses, which were constructed upon commanding positions, and often mounted with cannon. Many of these structures were yet standing, and were seen in every direction.

The sufferings and sacrifices of this population, has few parallels in the atrocities of civil war! He entered into no family in which he did not hear of thrilling recitals of the massacre of some branch of it by ferocious barbarians who carried fire and the sword through their settlements, or of some appalling scene of danger and suffering connected with its own history. This entire people for many years were exposed to constant alarm and agitation. Without knowledge or suspicion of the immediate approach of their ruthless foes, settlements were burst upon and devastated at one swoop, in blood and flames, while the same tragic scene was often renewed the succeeding night, by the same bands, in some other remote and equally unsuspecting community.

On the second evening after leaving Johnson Hall he [Elkanah] reached a miserable log tavern, six miles from old Fort Schuyler, which stood upon the site of the present city of Utica. This tour proved an important epoch in the public career of Mr. Watson, and I therefore present the original language of his Journal, in order more distinctly to present his views and opinions at that period.

Extract from the Journal: "Sept. 1788. - From Col. Sterling's I began to traverse the wilderness bordering upon the Indian territory. The road is almost impassable; I was upwards of three hours in reaching the Mohawk opposite old Fort Schuyler, a distance of only six miles. Here I reluctantly forded the river, being alone and without a guide, and both shores alive with savages. Having fasted twenty-four hours, in consequence of a severe head-ache the day previous, I was by this time excessively hungry and fatigued. As there was no tavern, and only a few scattering houses, I proceeded to an old German log house, on the margin of the river, and interceded for something to eat. At length, after much difficulty, I prevailed on an ill-natured German woman to spare me two ears of green corn and some salt. I never suffered more from hunger in all my wanderings, than I did in 1788, on the spot now occupied by the large and flourishing village of Utica.

"The road from thence to Whitesborough continued as bad as possible, obstructed by broken bridges, logs, and stumps, and my horse, at every step, sinking knee-deep in the mud. I remained one day recruiting at Judge White's log house, the founder of the settlement, and slept in his log barn, with horses and other animals.[1]

"Whitesborough is a promising new settlement, situated on the south side of the Mohawk river, in the heart of a fine tract of land, and is just in its transition from a state of nature into civilization. The settlement commenced only three years since. It is astonishing what efforts are making to subdue the dense and murky forest. Log houses are already scattered in the midst of stumps, half-burnt logs, and girdled trees. I observed, however, with pleasure, that their log barns are well-filled. A few years ago

---

[1] "It could hardly have been supposed within the range of possibility, that it would fall to my lot to march by the side of President Lansing, and head a procession of two hundred respectable farmers, in the presence of several thousand spectators, into a Church on this very spot, exactly thirty years after this occurrence, and there proclaim the premiums of an Agricultural Society, and address them as follows: 'It is now thirty years this month since I lodged in a log barn, belonging to Judge White, near the spot from which I am now addressing you. This blooming vale was then just emerging from a wilderness, and the bloody footsteps of our savage foe. Behold now an apparently old country, bearing on its surface the refinements of civilized life.'"

land might have been bought for a trifle; at present, the lots bordering upon the river have advanced to three dollars per acre, and those lying a few miles back, at one dollar per acre.

"Settlers are continually pouring in from the Connecticut hive, which throws off its annual swarms of intelligent, industrious, and enterprizing emigrants - the best qualified of any men in the world to overcome and civilize the wilderness. They already estimate three hundred brother Yankees on their muster list, and in a few years hence they will undoubtedly be able to raise a formidable barrier, to oppose the incursions of the savages in the event of another war.

"At Oriskany I passed a small tribe of two hundred Indians, the remnant of that once powerful Mohawk nation, which was the former terror and dread of the New England frontier. On ascending a hill, I approached the place where the intrepid Gen. Herkimer was drawn into a fatal ambush and miserably defeated, in 1777. Herkimer was a gallant, but inexperienced leader, and here perished, with nearly half his army, formed of the patriotic yeomanry of the Mohawk valley. Just before reaching this sanguinary battle-field, I met two Germans familiar with its incidents. They conducted me over the whole ground, and in corroboration of the fact, of which they assured me, that many of the slain, who were scattered through the woods, were never interred. I noticed numerous human bones, strewn upon the surface of the earth. This movement was intended to succor Fort Stanwix, then beseiged by St. Leger.

"I found myself, soon after leaving this consecrated spot, alone in the woods, in the midst of a band of Indians, "*as drunk as lords.*" They looked like so many evil spirits broken loose from Pandemonium. Wild, frantic, almost naked, and frightfully painted, they whooped, yelled, and danced around me in such hideous attitudes, that I was seriously apprehensive they would end the farce by taking off my scalp, by way of a joke. I had luckily picked up the the word *Sago*, the salute of friendship, of which I made copious application, constantly extending my hand to the most active among them, by whom it was cordially accepted.

"On my arrival at Fort Stanwix, I found the whole plain around the fort covered with Indians, of various tribes, male and female. Many of the latter were fantastically dressed in their best attire - in the richest silks, fine scarlet clothes, bordered with gold fringe, a profusion of brooches, rings in their noses, their ears slit,

Rome Historical Society

*Iroquois negotiating Fort Stanwix Treaty of 1784, drawn
by Howard C. Rohmer.*

and their heads decorated with feathers. Among them I noticed some very handsome contenances and fine figures.

"I luckily procured a sleeping-place in the garret of the house in which Gov. [George] Clinton and the eight other commissioners - also John Taylor, Esq., of Albany, Indian Agent-Egbert Benson, Esq., of New York, and a man with a large white wig, by the name of Dr. Taylor - were quartered. The sight of this wig fixed the attention, and excited the mirth of many of the Indians, one of whom I noticed making strong efforts to smother a laugh in the Doctor's face, since nothing could appear more ludicrous and grotesque to an Indian, than a bushy white wig.

"The object of this great treaty is to procure a cession from the Indians, of territory lying west of Fort Stanwix, in this State, and extending to the great lakes. Fort Stanwix was built in 1758, by the British Government, at a cost of £60,000, and is situated on an artificial eminence, near the river; a large area around it is entirely cleared. Here Col. Gansevoort, in 1777, sustained a terrible siege, until relieved by [Gen. Benedict] Arnold, when St. Leger made a precipitate retreat, abandoning most of his camp equipage and munitions. The French Ambassador, Count Moutier, and the Marchioness De Biron, are now encamped within the Fort, under a marque formerly used by Lord Cornwallis. This enterprising and courageous lady has exposed herself to the greatest fatigues and privations to gratify her unbounded curiosity, by coming all the way from the city of New York, to witness this great and unusual assemblage of savage tribes.

"In contemplating the position of Fort Stanwix, at the head of the bateaux navigation on the Mohawk river, within one mile of Wood Creek, which runs west towards Lake Ontario, I am led to think it will in time become the emporium of commerce between Albany and the vast Western world. Wood Creek is indeed small, but it is the only water communication with the great Lakes; it empties into the Oneida Lake, the outlet of which unites with the Onondaga and Oswego, and discharges into Lake Ontario at Fort Oswego, where the British have a garrison. Should the Little Falls be ever locked, the obstructions in the Mohawk river removed, and a canal between that river and Wood Creek at this place be formed, so as to unite the waters flowing east with those running west, and other canals made, and obstructions removed to Fort Oswego - who can reasonably doubt that by such bold operations, the State of New York has within her power, by a great measure of policy, to divert the future trade of Lake Ontario, and the great lakes above, from Alexandria and Quebec to Albany and New York?

"The object of the present treaty is the purchase of an immense territory, estimated at eight millions of acres, and now owned, and chiefly inhabited, by the Six Nations of Indians. The sovereignty of this tract has been in dispute between Massachusetts and New York. These States have at length made an amicable division, assigning four millions of acres to each. The former has since sold her right of domain to a company of adventurers, who have purchased preemption from the Indians. New York, by this treaty, has accomplished the same result. This vast territory therefore, is now opened without any impediments, to the flood of emigration which will pour into it from the East. Many hardy pioneers have already planted themselves among the savages; and it is probable that the enthusiasm for the occupation of new territory, which now prevails, will in the period of the next twenty years, spread over this fertile region a properous and vigorous population.

"I left Fort Stanwix with the intention of passing down Wood Creek to Lake Ontario, indulging the idea of extending my tour to Detroit. Under the strong presentiment that a canal communication will be opened, sooner or later, between the great lakes and the Hudson, I was anxious to explore its probably course. A hard rain commencing, and the obstacles I found to exist in the creek, induced me however to abandon the arduous enterprise, and return to Fort Stanwix. The attempt afforded me the gratification of sailing west for the first time, in the interior of America.

"I continued several days at the Treaty, passing my time most agreeably, in associating with the Commissioners, and much diverted, by the novel and amusing scenes exhibited in the Indian camp. The plain in the vicinity of the fort has already been laid out into a town plot; a few houses have been erected, and also saw mills, and other improvements, at a distance of a mile on Wood Creek.

"A young Indian, named Peter Otsequett, a Chief of the Oneidas, was also attending this Treaty: he had just returned from France, having been in that country for several years, under the patronage of the Marquis Lafayette, by whom he was taken when a boy. He is probably the most polished and best educated Indian in North America. He speaks both French and English accurately; is familiar with music and many branches of polite and elegant literature; and in his manners is a well-bred Frenchman. He is, however, a striking instance of the moral impracticability of civilizing an Indian. There appears to exist natural impediments to their amelioration. While visiting the Catawba Indians a year since, I became acquainted with a young Indian, who had been educated at a prominent college; but had already fallen into the degradation of his native savage habits, and was to all intents an Indian. It is noticed that each year, in its progress, wears off European polish of Otsequett, and brings him nearer the savage.* Ten days ago I was introduced to him, a polite and well-informed gentleman, today I beheld him splashing through the mud, in the rain, on horseback, with a young squaw behind him, both comfortably drunk.

"My curiosity satisfied, I sent my horse towards Albany, and embarked on board a returning bateau, and proceeded down the Mohawk to Little Falls, anxious to examine that place, with an eye to canals. We abandoned ourselves to the current of the river, which, with the aid of our oars, impelled us at a rapid rate. We met numerous bateaux coming up the river, freighted with whole families, emigrating to the 'land of promise.' I was surprised to observe the dexterity with which they manage their boats, and the progress they make in polling up the river, against a current of at least three miles an hour. The first night we encamped at a log-hut on the banks of the river, and the next morning I disembarked at German Flats.

---

* I have since been assured by a gentleman, who knew Otsequett near the close of his life, that he actually degenerated below the ordinary level of savages. His refined education in France, commencing when a boy, had divested him of those masculine virtues which are engrafted on the Indian character. Having lost these, he possessed no traits of high qualities to sustain him, and abandoning himself to the bottle, he ultimately became an abandoned vagabond. (1821)

TRAVELS

THROUGH

THE UNITED STATES

OF

NORTH AMERICA,

THE

COUNTRY OF THE IROQUOIS,

AND

UPPER CANADA,

IN THE YEARS 1795, 1796, AND 1797;

WITH AN AUTHENTIC ACCOUNT OF LOWER CANADA.

BY THE

DUKE DE LA ROCHEFOUCAULT
LIANCOURT.

London:

PRINTED FOR R. PHILLIPS, NO. 71, ST. PAUL'S CHURCH YARD,
SOLD BY T. HURST AND J. WALLIS, PATERNOSTER-ROW, AND BY CARPENTER AND CO.
OLD BOND STREET.

1799.

Travels Through Oneida County
in 1795

LAKE ONEIDA

Lake Oneida is twenty-eight miles in length. You see not one building or any settlement along the banks of the lake, excepting the farm house built by Mr. Vanderkamp and situated five miles east of Rodderdam [Constantia]. Endless forests and indifferent soil and no eminence appear towards the north. The country rises more southwards where the mountains come in view at the distance of ten or twelve miles in a direction parallel to the lake. Lake Oneida is from five to six miles in breadth. On the southeast bank, a few miles from the shore, stands the Indian village of Oneida. This nation is now engaged in concluding a treaty by which it is to sell the country south of Oneida Lake, called the Oneida Reservation, to the State of New York. I am not acquainted with the conditions of the treaty. All I know is that the nation is to retain a tract of land of twelve square miles in extent, which is secured to them by all possible means together with the right of free fishery in the lake. But a few years ago the Oneida Indians were possessors of an immense extent of country, which is now in the hands of the American speculators. These lands should come into such hands as are able to put them into a good condition, can be no matter of regret especially as the Indians consented to it. But might it not be possible to form settlements amidst these people to civilize them by agriculture and to instruct them by example? This tribe, it is asserted, increases rather than decreases in numbers. If it is true it would be the only instance among all the Indian nations and deserves encouragement. Civilization is said to have already, in some measure, gaining ground among the Indians. Agriculture has reached a higher degree of perfection with them than in any other tribe. The negotiation, we were informed, have met with obstructions, which is likely to impede a successful issue. General Schuyler, who conducts them on part of the United States, and who intends to purchase all the land on his own account, experiences a strong opposition from Timothy Pickering, the Secretary of State, who is said to be displeased that he himself cannot come in for a share in the proposed indemnifications. These particulars, which I have from persons who think themselves well informed, may yet be mere scandalous reports, although they carry no improbability with them.*

WOOD CREEK**

We counted on advancing a few miles on Wood Creek before we should stop, when we fell in with our company from Albany, who had halted at the mouth of the lake. A fit of Ague [malarial fever] had obliged Mr. Van Rensselaer to put an end to this days journey at two o'clock in the afternoon. The gentlemen proposed to us to stop likewise. Our conductor accepted the proposal and our consent was a matter of course. We spent the night in scratching rather than in sleep for mosquitoes and small gnats are more numerous and troublesome along the banks of Wood Creek than in any other part of these wilderness. We were obliged to send for water to a spring, which was known to the people on board our vessel, which was three miles away. This water, though bad in itself was excellent in comparison with the muddy and stagent water of Wood Creek, and with rum was drinkable. Our dinner consisted of some potatoes, which were left over from our last meal at Rotterdam. We had plenty of biscuit, and although we were badly off in every respect, yet we found that things might be worse.

Wood Creek is a small stream emptying into Lake Oneida. At its mouth it is scare sixteen yards in breath and somewhat farther up hardly eight. The course of this creek being a continued

* The negotiations mentioned by the author actually lead to the treaty of 1795 by which the Oneida nation sold the Oneida reservation to the State of New York for an annuity of three thousand five hundred and fifty two dollars. Translator.

** An earlier name was River Vilcrick.

Rome Historical Society

Wood Creek

serpentine wind, the distance from its source to the mouth, which in a straight line is estimated at fifteen miles, is trebled by these meanders. It is under contemplation to construct a canal which would cut off several of these windings and to retain part of its present channel. The moderate mass of water contained in this stream is also obstructed by a considerable number of trees rooted out and swept along by the stream in Spring and Autumn when it overflows its banks. It is with great difficulty a vessel works her way through these incumbrances. This sluggish river has probably taken its name from the great number of trunks of trees which obstruct the navigation and rot in the water for otherwise it has no better claim to the name wood creek than all other small rivers in America which in general flow through woods. The navigation is, in my opinion, far more troublesome than that of the Oswego river. The proposed canal, were it ever finished and kept in good repair, should for ever remove the impediments which obstruct navigation. Throughout the whole course of this creek it receives only the waters of Canada Creek, which excepting two months of the year, discharges into it but a small quantity of water. In the spring it rises in so extraordinary degree that the trees under which we are now passing along and the branches of which hang two feet over our heads were last May covered with water in such a manner that the same vessel in which we now find ourselves at that time passed over trees without noticing their existence.

CANADA CREEK

On arrival of vessels in Canada Creek they must be unloaded to pass nine or ten miles farther, the last two miles cannot be passed at all if the miller, who possesses a mill at the entrance of the creek, allow not his water to flow into the creek, which he sometimes refuses to do. The cargoes of the vessels are transported in wagons. The vessels themselves, when they approach the source of wood Creek, are put on wagons to pass the interval which separate the lake we have left from the Mohawk River where they are launched again.

Although our party had formed the bold resolution of pushing on to the Mohawk River we halted at Canada Creek resolved to let the vessels proceed onward in moonshine and to pursue the voyage the next morning at break of day. The soil was all along of a black colour and excellent quality although it did not cover the rocky ground to any considerable depth.

In the whole course of our navigation on Wood Creek we saw not one building and found but one spring, called Oak Orchard, which was four minutes filling a small glass and the water of which was but of a middling quality.

FORT STANWIX

In the evening we generally say "we shall be awake early in the morning" but this frequently is not the case. A fatiguing journey is protected in a tedious manner and a good night's lodging is seldom obtained in a country where in general such lodging is exceedingly rare. This inconvenience, however, cannot possibly be avoided by a numerous party composed by people labouring under infernities and fond of ease. Our vessels had not yet started at six in the morning; the wagons had not yet arrived and it was seven o'clock before we left Mr. Gilbert's inn, which we found tolerably good and which would have been much better had our company been less numerous. Rotterdam we had left full of sick people. We were now about fifty miles from it and had seen no house. The first house we entered was no less an infirmary. The landlady, the maid, the man-servant were all indisposed with the ague. The few neighbours of the inn were in the same situation as the Gilbert family.

The land along Wood Creek, which is not of great value, being subject to inundation, costs three dollars an acre. The price about Gilbert's house is five dollars and it is but of middling quality. The construction of the canal induces the proprietors to raise the price of the land, though it is not frequently sought after and in truth I am at a loss to conceive how any can be tempted to inhabit the banks of this miserable creek.

Messrs. Van Rensselaer and Van Allen, the two sick members of our party made the tour on horseback. Mr. Henry, Mr. Stouts and myself traveled on foot. Dupetitthouars, passionately fond of vessels and navigation followed the boats to help them along.

The whole tract of country through which this river flows is called Fort Stanwix and takes its name from a fort erected for the protection of the communication between the two ends of the river. Colonel St. Leger, in order to attack this fort, attempted the difficult navigation of Wood Creek, still more obstructed by

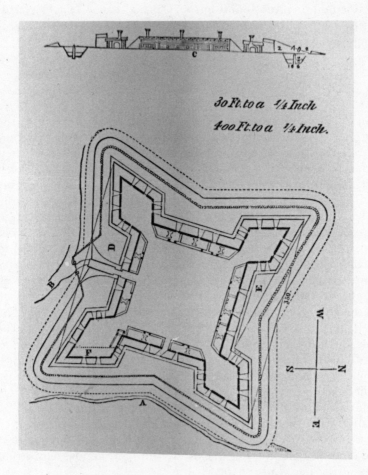

30 Ft. to a ¼ Inch.
400 Ft. to a ¼ Inch.

Rome Historical Society

Fort Stanwix

trees, which the Americans had purposely thrown into the stream. He succeeded in penetrating to the fort, which he besieged but the intelligence of the capture of General Burgoyne's army put a speedy end to the siege. I learned from General Simcoe that on this retreat the English troops lost more men from Indians firing on them than from the pursuit of the Americans. We halted on the spot where Wood Creek entirely ceases to be navigable, very near to its source.

The inn of Mr. Sterney was full of people indisposed with the ague. The whole neighborhood was crowded with others in the same condition, and, by his account, numbers of travelers are daily arriving who have not escaped the influence of the tainted air and the contagion which prevails in the district of Genesee. Within this past fortnight the flux [dysentery] has joined the fever, already sufficiently dreadful in itself. It rages with all the violence of an epidemical disease and carried off a great many people. At every door, at which we stopped, we observed the same yellow paleness in every face and received the same accounts.

Having at length reached the place on the river Mohawk where we were to embark we found Mr. Rensselaer in a fit of the ague. An hour after arrived the mate of Mr. Van Allen's vessel seized with the same illness and, last of all, came Dupetitthouars, the Hercules of our party, complaining of pains in his limbs, headache and cold shiverings. The poor man had felt the symptoms these two days but concealed it from me less I should repeat my earnest entreaties to him not to continue. Every one of our party, who felt not quite sick, began now to examine whether he were not deceived in his opinion of being well. The fear of being attacked by the universal contagion was openly confessed and the whole conservation turned upon the means of escaping it; on the most wholesome foods and the best remedies. Our whole day was spent in this manner for our vessels, which had set out at seven o'clock in the morning, did not arrive until nine in the evening. The great number of the sick in the country, attention to the patients of our own party, and waiting for the vessels prevented me from collecting information. What little intelligence I obtained is as follows: the land of the Mohawk River costs five dollars an acre. The settlers in this township, which was formed six or seven years ago, come mostly from Connecticut. Among these are Methodists, Baptists and Episcopalians but the major part are Presbyterians. Divine service is performed in private houses and pretty regularly attended. From want of preachers all the prayers are read successively by a member of the congregation and this consists of the whole service.

MAYER'S TAVERN - MOHAWK RIVER

I had cherished a hope that Dupetitthouars' sufferings would be finished in half a day and that this would be the only punishment for the excessive fatigue which he had imprudently undergone. But the ague has actually made its appearance with all the symptoms which characterize this malady. Our situation is extremely unpleasant unprovided as we are with any means of assistance. Although exhausted by fatique and scorched by the sun from which nothing can protect us in this vexatious vessel we have not yet been in a bed these eight days past. Independently of my apprehension for my companions I most devoutly wish to see the end of this passage yet our arrival in Albany is continually delayed by new obstructions.

The navigation of the Mohawk River is fortunately not like the rivers we have passed lately. We descended gently with the stream and although its channel is in some places obstructed with trees they may be easily cleared. It receives many small creek and springs, the water of which is excellent. The soil is good all along the way we have traveled but grows better in proportion as you proceed to a greater distance from the source of the stream. The settlements are more numerous especially on the right bank. Ten miles farther on they begin likewise to be found on the left bank. Communications between the settlers on both sides is kept up by wooden bridges.

Ten miles from Fort Stanwix the price of land is from five to six dollars per acre. A great part is leased out for life, the lessee agrees to pay the proprietor a certain sum per acre as long as he cultivates it. The lease is generally granted for three lives which he can choose at pleasure, or for his life and the lives of his children. The man in whose house we breakfasted hold one hundred acres by this tenure. Only nineteen acres has been cleared for he settled here only fifteen months ago. Ten of these acres are sown with wheat yielding from thirty to thirty-five bushels an acre which affords him not only subsistence but also a sufficient overplus to pay his rent.

THE

DOCUMENTARY HISTORY

OF THE

STATE OF NEW-YORK;

ARRANGED UNDER DIRECTION OF THE

Hon. CHRISTOPHER MORGAN,
Secretary of State.

BY E. B. O'CALLAGHAN, M. D.

VOL. III.

——————◆——————

ALBANY:
WEED, PARSONS & Co., PUBLIC PRINTERS
......
1850.

Journal of Rev. John Taylor's Missionary Tour

The Rev. John Taylor (1762-1840) graduated from Yale in 1784. In 1802, he was called by the Missionary Society of Hampshire County, Massachusetts to engage in missionary work in New York State. He left Albany on the 21st of July 1802 and arrived at Utica July 29th and remained in Oneida County for almost a month.

(Vol. III The Documentary History of the State of New York, Albany; Weed, Parsons & Co., 1850)

July 29th - Left Norway for Utica, about 22 miles to the southwest. In passing out of this town. I saw a daughter of Mr. Joshua Sweet - appears to be comfortably situated. About 3 miles from the center of Norway, we go down from the uplands, and come upon White Creek, a very useful stream. Here the hills are rugged. We rise from the creek again into uplands - pass on a few miles, and go down upon Canada creek. After crossing the river, we begin to rise a mountain which is patent land. We go on 10 miles through this mountain, which is the highest in those parts - but all good passable land. At the foot of this mountain, we enter into a corner of the town of Skyler. From thence we go about 6 miles to the river road - pass a few miles in Deerfield and pass the Mohawk into Utica. This is a very pleasant and beautiful village.

Utica appears to be a mixed mass of discordant materials. Here may be found people of ten, or 12 different nations, and of almost all religions and sects; but the greatest part are of no religion. The world is the great object with this body of people. I put up at Mr. Baggs' - saw the lady of the Hon. C. Phelps, Esq. on her way from Canadaigua to Suffield, in a common Dutch wagon, covered with tow cloth. My health is good - something wearied with travelling. Determined to visit Norway on my return home.

30th - From Utica to Whitesborough, is 4 miles - pleasant riding. Whitesborough is not so large and flourishing a place as I expected to find. It is, however, a pleasant village. Dined at Dr. Mosley's. In the afternoon rode out 9 miles to Clinton.

Most churches in this part of the world are on the presbyterian plan. The church at Clinton is, however, congregational. Mr. Norton has a church containing 240 members; and this people is considered to be most harmonious, regular and pious of any in the northern part of the State of New York. In this town, or rather parish, is an academy, which is a flourishing state. A Mr. Porter, an excellent character, and a preacher, is preceptor. They have one usher, and about 60 scholars. This institution promises fair to be of great service to this part of the country. There is in the town a few Universalists, and one small baptist church but not a sufficient number to have any influence. In the society of Paris, of which Clinton is a part, Mr. Steel is pastor; he is said to be a good, and reputable man - he has a respectable congregation. In Hanover, a society of Paris, Mr. Bogue is Pastor.

North, or N.W. of Paris is Westmoreland - vacant - congregation considerably divided. Sangersfield lies south - congregationalist.

Clinton is a flouishing place. The land is the best I have seen since I left home, and is the best tilled. The people are principally from Connecticut. On my way to this town, saw Capt. Mitchel, and his daughter who married a Rice. Meeting with Mitchel and his family was a pleasing scene. In all this part of the country there is no waste land; and indeed the original Whitestown - appears to be the garden of the world. Was treated with the greatest kindness and attention in Capt. Mitchel's family - which, as far as I am able to judge, is in a good situation. His farm is now in the bloom, and its appearance is pleasing.

31st - Parted with my good friend Mitchel and his family - returned back to Whitesborough - spent the afternoon very agreeably and profitably with Mr. Dodd, the minister.

August 1st, Sunday - Preached for Mr. Dodd in a schoolhouse. Audience devout, and attentive - a great mixture of people, as respects nations, and religions.

Afternoon at Utica - put up with Lawyer Clark from Lebanon. There is but a handful of people in this place who have much regard for preaching, or for anything but the world. 8 years last spring there were but 2 houses in the present town plot. There is now above 90 - Lodge at Baggs'.

August 2nd. - Started for Floyd - rode 11 miles to a Capt.

Rice's. Preached in the evening. I know not what remarks to make upon the inhabitants of this town - a half a dozen excepted, they seem to be the fag-end [lower quality] of man in disorder, and confusion of all kinds. The baptists have some regularity; but the methodists are producing the scenes which are transpiring in Kentucky. Here methodist's women pray in their families instead of the men - and with such strength of lungs as to be distinctly heard by their neighbors. I had almost as many nations, sects, and religions present to hear me preach, as Peter had on the day of Pentecost. In this town there is an excellent character, Est. Dier - he tells me that [Governor] Clinton has given commissions to 5 men for Justices, in this place - one of whom is a renegade Irishman, without character and without prayer; and the other has no bible in his house. In fact, this is a most miserable place, - as to inhabitants. The land is good - too good for such inhabitants.

3rd and 4th - At Trenton. This town is a part of the Holland Patent. Boon's settlement is within the circle of this town. The land is tolerable - some of it very good - well watered - about 130 voters. Found on the high land, rocks and stones containing sea shells petrified into stone, and forming parts of stones. This is another evidence that the Mohawk at the Little Falls was once obstructed by the rocks - and that the lands in this town were a part of a large lake. Timber - beech, maple, ash, birch, and bass.

5th - 10th - STEUBEN. This patent is on the height of land between the Mohawk and the Black river - some of the head-waters of both are in this town. Standing on a hill, near the center of the town, we have an extensive prospect on 3 sides; - to the N.W., about 35 miles, we see the Oneida Lake - south we see the settlements of New Hartford and Clinton - Clinton Academy is in full view. We can here see the tops of the Catskill mountains. It is said that upon the tops of the trees Ontario is in sight. Upon this height of land, I found in a number of places sea shells which form constituent parts of rocks and stones. This land is so high that this singular fact cannot be accounted for by supposing that the rocks at the Little Falls, were once united; for this land is evidently much higher than the mountain at that place. The face of the country is here rough and uncouth; something stony - yet no hills so steep as to render any land useless. Between this and Clinton is about 4 miles of low flat land - very rich, and heavy timbered. Unsettled but a very little part of this county is settled.

O'Callaghan, Documented History of New York State, Vol. III

Baron Steuben's Residence, 1802

A considerable part of the lands which are settled, are to hire on lease - the inhabitants have not the right of soil. 10 shillings is the common price for 100 acres annual rent; but most of these leases are for perpetuity. About 1/3 of the people in Steuben are Welch - who are industrious and prudent beyond all example. I am now at the house of the first settler who came into the town, Esq. Siser's.

Here I find the grave of the once active and enterprising STEUBEN. He lies in a swamp, under a Hemlock, with a bier standing over the grave, and a few rough boards nailed to some trees to keep the cattle off. Alas! what is man! that the great STEUBEN should be suffered to lie in such a place - and without a decent monument.

A few rods from this swamp, we find the place of his former residence - of which I have taken a rough drawing. This is a very healthful situation. The house faces the south - and there is a gradual descent for about 80 rods, and an opening about 50 rods wide. The seat of this great man was not indeed a palace, nor what we should suppose would afford contentment to the mind of an enterprising nobleman: It consists of 2 log houses - one at the end of the other - containing in the whole 3 rooms - unsealed. It is, however, a decent loghouse. The Baron died in a fit of numb palsy.

Crops in this town much injured by rust. Winter wheat is open to winter kill - the lands, though high, are very wet. There is, however, some low, rich land, of the nature of marsh. The prospect on the height of land in this town is extensive.

WESTERN, Wednesday, 11th. - In passing from Steuben west, we descend for about 2 miles - and come to a branch of the Mohawk - and pass a tract of excellent land - heavy timbered, and well watered. In about 2 miles from this Eastern settlement in this town, we come to another settlement, in which we find Gen. Floyd, one of the signers of Independence, and one of the members of Congress during the whole of the American war with Great Britain. He is about 70 years of age - retains in full his powers of mind. He spends the summers in this place, and the winters on his seat on Long Island. He is a gentleman of immense property: and is now building an elegant seat upon the banks of the Mohawk.

It is incredible how thick this part of the world is settled - and what progress is making in opening the wilderness and turning it into a fruitful plain. The land in this town is most excellent -

crops are rich. The same evil operates here, however, as in many parts of this country - the lands are most of them leased. This must necessarily operate to debase the minds and destroy the enterprise of the settlers - although the rent is small - only 19 an acre; yet if men do not possess the right of soil, they never will, nor can, feel independent. And what is as great an evil, they will always be under the influence of their landlords.

August 12th, - Preached to a congregation principally Methodists - 2 methodist preachers present. Put up with Gen. Floyd, who informs me that the methodists are making great strides, and appear to be doing some good as well as much hurt. Previous to their meetings the Sabbath was almost wholly disregarded by the great body of the people, and they were but little removed from the heathenish state; but that now, whatever disorders there may be in their meetings, they appear to have become moral in all their conduct, and to be impressed in their minds with a sense of Divine things. Gen. Floyd thinks that many of the best characters among them, when they have had time to reflect, and when their passions are a little subsided; will fall off from this sect, and will become presbyterians or congregationalists. At present he thinks that they ought to be treated with great tenderness.

Friday, 13th. - Passed on 4 miles to the west to a settlement on the bend of the Mohawk - a flat and rich country - land here a black loam; - it is a meadow, and much of it is made ground [cultivated]. Crossed the Mohawk, and put up with Esq. Wicks - treated with the greatest respect. A woman by the name of Anderson called to see me - also a Mr. Wills, originally from Shelburn. In this part of the county may be found all the shades of character, from the most ignorant and abandoned, to the most virtuous and excellent. Society is in a miserable state - it is, however, progressing on towards order. There is a mixture of all sects, which will undoubtedly for a long time retard religious order. In consequence of the imprudence of the methodists, and their erroneous sentiments, party spirit in matters of religion, it is to be feared, will soon arise. In this town there is one congregational church.

Saturday, 14th. - Rode 3 miles to the west. The face of the country level, and excellent - heavy timbered. Inhabitants very thick - log-houses may be found in every direction. The people appear to be cheerful, and are all under the influence of a hope of better times - the happiest situation, I believe that men can be in. Over all the face of this country, may be found in great plenty the petrified sea shells - some in rocks, and some in stones. Timber - is beech and maple, generally; some ash, and a little bass.

Monday, 16th. - At. Mr. Lord's - who has 2 sisters with him - all of whom are children of Benjamin Lord of Norwich - and are my cousins. They are comfortably situated - have a good farm, and a good framed house. The west part of Western is in a fine tract of land, and many of the inhabitants are good characters, and persons of some property.

Tuesday, 17th. - At Eli Bush's - in the Northwest corner of the town. All his children but one are with him; and he is in a flourishing situation, and appears to enjoy himself well. A mile and a half west is Fish creek, which supplies all this part of the world with the best of salmon. The people are not allowed to take them with seins, but stabs. This river is peculiar. The banks, for miles, are almost perpendicular - and are from 50 to 150 feet above the water. It is very rapid, and rocky. It arises from a pond in which the salmon spawn. This part of the town is on high lands; yet the ascent is so gradual as hardly to be perceivable. We are now in sight of the Oneida lake.

The sea shells, petrified into stones, are very thick on this land. Face of the country very pleasant. Crops of corn, oats, and grass, equal if not superior to any I have seen. Water pure. It is, in fact, a noble country, and needs nothing but clearing to make it a fruitful garden. However strange it may appear, yet it is a fact, goods of all kinds are cheaper here than in the county of Hampshire. Salt is 7/6 - or by the barrel 6/.

ROME, Wednesday, 18th, at Esq. Hathaway's. This is a pleasant village, upon the banks of the Mohawk. The old Fort Stanwix stands about 30 rods from the river. It is regularly built: the intrenchment is very deep. In the centre of the fort stands the old block house.

It is a very great singularity, that the waters of the Mohawk and those of Wood Creek, which run in opposite directions, should here come within a mile of each other - and should admit of a communication by water through canals. This communication is of incalculable benefit to this part of the world. Produce may be sent both ways. Sunday, after meeting, took tea at Pease's. - He appears to be a man of business, and is gaining property. He has a family, and a sister with him, who appears to be a very likely person.

CAMDEN, August 23rd. - 22 miles N.W. of Rome. This town began to settle about five years since; contains about 80 families. Some of the land very excellent. Here is pine timber. Soil is a black loam in general. There is in this town, which includes six original towns, some sandy hills, and some oak timber. There is a variety of lands in this town. There are 2 settlements, which have unfortunately separated as to public worship. Good mills on a branch of Fish creek. I have now got into the wilderness indeed; - the openings are small - the people rub hard - some of them feel a want of the necessaries of life.

TRAVELS

ON

AN INLAND VOYAGE

THROUGH THE

STATES OF NEW-YORK, PENNSYLVANIA, VIRGINIA,
OHIO, KENTUCKY AND TENNESSEE,

AND THROUGH

THE TERRITORIES OF INDIANA, LOUISIANA,
MISSISSIPPI AND NEW-ORLEANS;

PERFORMED

IN THE YEARS 1807 AND 1808;

INCLUDING A TOUR OF NEARLY SIX THOUSAND MILES.

WITH MAPS AND PLATES.

BY CHRISTIAN SCHULTZ, JUN. ESQ.

IN TWO VOLUMES.....VOL. I.

NEW-YORK :

Printed by Isaac Riley.

1810.

C. Schultz, Jun.r

Published by I. Riley, 1810.

Travels through Oneida Co. in 1807

Utica, Mohawk River, July 15, 1807

AGREEABLY to your request and my promise, I now commence sketching, for your amusement, the few hasty observations I have made on my voyage to this place; yet, as these will neither be very new nor interesting to you, who are equally well-informed as to the state of improvements thus far, I shall occasionally introduce such little incidents as may occur on my voyage, being satisfied with the sincerity of your avowal, that "any thing from me will be acceptable."

You desired me to be particular in describing the several towns and streams I pass on my route, the respective distances between them, the time occupied and manner of travelling from one to another, as well as an account of the expenses, risks and dangers to be incurred in an inland voyage of the kind I am now performing. All these I shall endeavour to attend to in their proper time and place; and, should I fail in affording you all the satisfaction or amusement you may have anticipated, it will not be from want of any exertion on my part.

Utica, on the site of Fort Schuyler, is a flourishing village, handsomely situated on the left bank of the Mohawk; it contains, at present, about one hundred and sixty houses, the greatest part of which are painted white, and give it a neat and lively appearance. Foreign goods are nearly as cheap here as in New-York, which, I presume, is owing to the merchants' underselling each other; for this, like all other country towns is overstocked with shop-keepers. Most of the goods intended for the salt-works are loaded here in wagons, and sent on over land, a distance of fifty miles. The carriage over this portage is fifty cents a hundred weight.

Whitestown is also a thriving little village, four miles above Utica; but, as it stands about half a mile back from the shore, nothing of it is seen in the passage up the river. Deerfield lies on the right bank of the Mohawk immediately opposite to Utica, and is connected with it by a good wooden bridge. It is but an inconsiderable village, of eight or ten houses, chiefly inhabited by very poor people; nor is it likely ever to rise to any degree of respectability, as the ground on which it is situated is subject to be overflowed whenever there is any considerable rise of the river.

The Mohawk affords the fewest fish of any stream I have ever yet met with. Angling, you know, is my favourite sport; and, as I had promised myself much gratification from this amusement, I spared nothing that could render my fishing apparatus complete; judge then of my patience and disappointment, when, after nine day's toiling, day and night, I at last caught a poor cat fish not larger than a herring!! I hope, however, in a few days, to be amply compensated for my disappointment here, as we shall then be at the head of the Mohawk, and from thence descend with the waters flowing into Lake Ontario, which our captain informs me abounds with salmon and other delicious fish; yet, even here, I perceive, another difficulty presents itself, which is, that nature has been so bountiful to the salmon of this country, in furnishing them with quantities of delicious food, as to make them reject the very best tid-bit you can affix to your hook; so that, unless you are expert enough to strike them with a spear, as is the custom, you are likely to go without. I really must confess that my feelings seem rather to revolt at the barbarous and unnatural idea of murdering fish with a large piece of iron, weighing three or four pounds, while, at the same time, a little bit of crooked steel, covered with a fly or worm, and suspended to the line, would afford me, for hours, what I should call rational amusement. Such is the force of habit and prejudice! The manly attitude of the Indian, standing erect in his canoe as he skims the transparent surface of the lake, grasping his iron spear with his right hand, warns the quick-eyed salmon of his hostile approach - while we, more humane and refined, conceal ourselves under the thick foliage of the shady banks, and, in the guise of friendship, beguile the unwary tribe to the deceitful hook!

Lake Ontario, Oswego, July 24, 1807.

MY last, I think, left me moralizing in consequence of my disappointments in fishing on the Mohawk: I shall not say another word upon that subject, for, to be candid, the first "glorious nibble" I afterward had, banished all unpleasant ideas respecting the past.

At Utica I made some little improvements in our boat, which consisted of an awning sufficiently large to secure us pretty comfortable from the rain and sun. The passage from Utica to this place [Lake Ontario], a distance of one hundred and fourteen miles, occupied nine days, two of which, however, were spent at Three River Point in waiting for me, as I had resolved not to miss the opportunity of visiting the famous salt-works of Onondago. The freight to this place is at the rate of one dollar and twenty-five cents per hundred. The passage money, if any is charged, is about two dollars for a hundred miles, finding your own provisions; but, if you furnish a good table, no passage money will be received; and these open-hearted fellows always seem much pleased to have gentlemen for passengers.

Rome, which lies in latitude 43. 12. N. and 75. 27. W. is situated near the head of the Mohawk, sixteen miles above Utica. The entrance into this village is through a handsome canal about a mile in length. It is here that the Mohawk is made to contribute a part of its stream toward filling Wood Creek, which, of itself, is so low in dry seasons as to be totally insufficient to float a boat without the aid of the Mohawk. Rome, formerly known as Fort Stanwix, is delightfully situated in an elevated and level country, commanding an extensive view for about ten miles around. This village consists at present of about eighty houses; but it seems quite destitute of every kind of trade, and rather on the decline. The only spirit which I perceived stirring among them was that of money digging; and the old fort betrayed evident signs of the prevalence of this mania, as it had literally been turned inside out for the purpose of discovering concealed treasure.

In proceeding from the Mohawk through the canal into Wood Creek, and descending the same, you pass through another range of locks, five in number. The toll here is still higher than the first, being three dollars per ton for goods, and from one dollar and fifty cents to three dollars and fifty cents extra upon each boat. This charge is usually paid by the boatman who takes the freight; but I am informed that it is necessary to come to an understanding on this point at the time of making the contract, as this expense is sometimes thrown upon the shipper.

Wood Creek is a narrow, crooked and sluggish stream, about twenty-four miles in length, from its head at Rome to its junction with the Oneida lake, and about twelve yards wide after passing through the locks. It winds through a low swampy tract of country from eight to ten miles in length, and four or five in breadth. Although this stream is celebrated for the size, activity and numbers of its moschetoes, as well as the stagnancy of its waters, yet I neither experienced the annoyance of the one, nor the inconvenience of the other, although I passed it in the month of July, when both these evils are said to be intolerable. Just after passing the store-house, which is situated below the last lock, a considerably rapid stream, called Canada Creek, unites with Wood Creek from the right. This is nearly as large as the former, but not navigable. Immediately opposite their junction are the remains of Fort Rickey, a fortress of some consequence during the old Indian wars; but at present employed to a better purpose, being covered with a good orchard. About a mile farther we passed the site of another old fort called Fort Bull; this is on the right bank of the creek. The navigation of Wood Creek is not attended with any hazard of drowning, or even of staving a boat to pieces; but the sudden turns of the stream overhung with the trunks and branches of trees, are not without their dangers, as I experienced. The boat being under considerable way, at a sudden bend of the river, we unexpectedly discovered a tree, which had been overturned by some late storm, stretched across the stream, and supported by its branches in such a manner as not to touch the water. Our captain immediately perceiving that it would be impossible to stop the boat in so short a distance, directed every one to take care of himself, and ran the boat under a part of the tree of sufficient height to admit it; but, as it was much lumbered up a-mid-ships, several of the articles were swept overboard. Amongst these were my travelling trunk and portable desk, containing my money, papers and apparel. The desk floated along side, but the trunk, being very heavy, sunk to the level of the water and stopped against some of the branches. As it required some time, however, to stop the boat and go up the stream, the trunk, on being taken up, was full of water, to the no little injury of my papers and clothing. The most laughable circumstance attending this accident was, that on missing my companion, and looking round for him, I discovered him in the top of the tree which we had passed under, whither he had jumped to avoid being crushed, as he had not time to get aft where the boat was less lumbered.

There is great plenty and a variety of fine fish in this stream; and, as we are now provided with the necessary cooking apparatus, I find, for the first time, my favourite amusement likely to be attended with profit. We have already seen several salmon jumping, but have not been able to catch any, except with a silver hook; nor should we, probably, have so soon been successful in this way had we not fortunately fallen in with a party of Oneida Indians, who were returning from fishing, and had two canoes loaded with fine salmon. Several of them weighed thirty pounds each. We purchased two of the largest for one dollar and twenty-five cents.

We stopped the same evening at a settlement a little distance above the mouth of Wood Creek, in order to obtain a fresh supply of milk for our coffee and chocolate. The sun had just set as we were ascending the bank, when we heard the cry of a hog in distress, and, upon approaching the house, found it was occasioned by a bear, who had come upon much the same errand with ourselves, namely, to get something to eat; but, as he found no one with whom to make a bargain, he very deliberately seized a small hog of about three hundred pounds weight, and marched off into the woods. By the time we came to the house we discovered an old woman, with a frying pan in one hand, and a ladle in the other, running after the robber; but she soon returned, and informed us that "this was the second time "the darnation devil had visited them within a "week."

Wood Creek is joined on the right by Fish Creek, which, with more propriety, might be denominated a river, as it is at least five times as large as Wood Creek, but navigable for ten miles only. This stream is much resorted to by the Oneida Indians, on account of the great quantities of salmon and other fish which it affords; as, likewise, from its being favoured with numerous springs of excellent water, which, in this country, is considered as a very great luxury.

About a mile and a half below the mouth of Fish Creek, the collected waters of these two streams are discharged into the Oneida Lake, where are still to be seen the remains of Fort Royal, formerly a post of considerable importance in checking the roving parties of Indians on this part of the frontier.

Oneida Lake is a most charming and beautiful sheet of water, about thirty miles in length, and five in breadth, and, I believe, affords the best and greatest variety of fish of any water in the western part of this state. I have seen salmon, pike and cat fish taken in this lake from five to thirty-five pounds weight, and chub, Oswego bass and white bass from two to five pounds; besides a great variety of smaller and less esteemed fish. Eels are found here in the greatest abundance, and are the finest and largest that ever I saw. They have an invention for taking them similar to our eel-pots, but made very large and requiring no bait. These are always set in a strong current, either at the inlet or outlet of a lake, or on some swift part of the stream upon the rivers. Two ridges of stones are piled up in the manner before described on the Mohawk river, at the lower end of which the pot or basket is set. I was present when one of the baskets, which had been set over night, was taken up; it filled two barrels, and the greater part of the eels weighed from two to three pounds each. I have been always prejudiced against eating eels on account of a rancid taste which I perceived in them; but, being prevailed upon to taste of these, I must declare that I never before tasted any fish so delicious, without excepting even the salmon. A family who live at the outlet of this lake, depend almost entirely upon this eel-fishery for their support; they salt down about forty barrels a year and find a ready sale for them at ten dollars a barrel.

The Oneida Indians, from whom this lake derives its name, are generally settled in this neighbourhood. We had, occasionally, met with one or two families of them previously to our arrival at the lake, but here we found a collection of about forty, who were amusing themselves with shooting arrows, pitching quoits, and throwing large stones. We made a stop here for the night, and found them all remarkably civil and well disposed.

There is a tolerably good tavern kept at this place by a Mrs. J_____, and her sister, a young woman, who, you may be assured, display no ordinary degree of courage in dealing out whiskey to thirty or forty Indians, who generally rendezvous at this place, especially as there is no other white settler within sight or call, should any accident render immediate assistance necessary. I made a small excursion along the border of this lake, and, although the shore was low, yet I found a firm, dry, white sandy beach to walk upon; some other parts of it, however, I was informed, were low and swampy. I was much amused in the evening by a singular illumination upon the lake, which I was at first wholly unable to account for. The water at this part of the lake, it seems, is very shallow for nearly half a mile from the shore, and being perfectly transparent, and the bottom a white sand, the smallest object may be readily distinguished. The Indians have a method of taking salmon and other fish by means of an iron frame fixed in the bow of the canoe, projecting forward three or four feet, and elevated about five; upon this they kindle a bright fire of pine knots, and while one person sits in the stern with a paddle to impel the boat forward, another stands in the bow with a sharp spear ready to strike the fish who play about the light. Ten or twelve of these canoes moving about irregularly on the lake, on a fine calm evening, with the reflection of their lights, like so many lines of fire, extending from each object to a centre on which you stand, afford a most pleasing prospect, and far exceed, in my opinion, the most brilliant display of artificial fireworks.

In crossing this lake we were fortunate enough to be favoured with a fair wind, and five hours' sailing brought us to the outlet, or head of Onondaga River. On our passage we had a tolerably fair view of Rotterdam, [Constantia], situated on the right bank of the lake, about six miles above the outlet. The country, generally, around the lake, and particularly in the neighbourhood of Rotterdam, has the character of being unhealthy, although the situation of the town appeared to me to be sufficiently elevated. Should the vicinity of these low and swampy grounds be the only cause of this unhealthyness, I am of opinion that a few hundred dollars expended, in opening the channel and removing the bar at the head of the outlet, would lower the lake so far as to drain off the stagnant waters, and thus remove the cause. I had an opportunity of examining the whole length of the bar by wading across it, and found it composed of loose stones and gravel, with no more than eighteen inches of water. Unless, therefore, there should prove to be a bed of rocks to impede the undertaking, I am inclined to believe that twenty men, with the necessary implements, might easily accomplish it in the course of a month.

As the wind would not permit us to stop at Rotterdam, I can only speak of it from information. It is said to contain about thirty houses, but mostly deserted, on account of what they call the lake fever, which, I am told, makes its appearance annually. There is an excellent set of mills built upon a stream called Bruce's Creek, which passes just below the town; and, although the country is extremely fertile, yet, for want of settlers to raise grain, they have but little employment. About four miles from the outlet we passed two islands on our left, sufficiently high for cultivation, and containing about one hundred acres, but destitute of inhabitants. We also passed a little spot called One Tree Island, which serves the navigators as a land-mark, and, at a distance, has the appearance of a ship under sail. There are likewise two small sandy islands, generally covered with gulls; the boatmen sometimes stop here to look for eggs, which, in the season, are found in considerable plenty. In passing these islands we ran aground on the top of what appeared to me to be a sunken island, with a very small flat surface; it was an entire rock, not more than seven paces across; and, on every side, we found more than thirty feet water, that being the length of the cord I sounded with.

It is astonishing what myriads of small butterflies covered the whole surface of this lake, which, indeed, rather resembled the large fields of an orchard, just spread with the fall of the blossoms. I had remarked that, at the head of the lake, one of the boatmen was directed to fill a keg with water before we started. I inquired for what reason, as the lake was fresh, and there was no danger of our being without water. I was informed that, at this season, "the lake was in blossom, and "the water full of fever and ague seeds, therefore "not fit to be drank." This I found almost literally true. The cause is as follows: - The lake is, in a great measure, bordered with swamps and low grounds, which produce innumerable swarms of small butterflies, especially of the white moth. These insects cannot fly any great distance without resting, and a very light breeze off shore will prevent their regaining the land when once they have taken wing; in consequence of which, they soon fall with outspread wings, and cover the lake so completely as fully to justify the expression of its being "in blossom." Although the water of the lake, before taken up in a glass, appears to be perfectly clear and transparent, yet, upon examination, it will be found to be full of small particles, which the boatmen call fever and ague seeds; but, in reality, are the eggs of certain insects. This inconvenience, however, continues only for about six weeks, when the waters again become pure and wholesome.

THE

LIFE AND WRITINGS

OF

DE WITT CLINTON,

BY

WILLIAM W. CAMPBELL,

AUTHOR OF " BORDER WARFARE OF NEW YORK, OR ANNALS
OF TRYON COUNTY."

———•———

New York:

BAKER AND SCRIBNER,
145 NASSAU ST., AND 36 PARK ROW.

1849.

Journal of DeWitt Clinton for 1810

The New York State legislature during March 1810 appointed a commission consisting of DeWitt Clinton, Governeur Morris, Stephen Van Rennssler, Simeon DeWitt, W. North, Thomas Eddy, Robert R. Livingston and Benjamin Wright of Rome as chief engineer to explore for a route to build a canal connecting Buffalo and Albany. The commission left Albany of the 3rd of July 1810 and arrived at Utica on the 10th.

UTICA

The Board met, all present, and adjourned to meet at Rome on the 12th instant.

Utica is a flourishing village on the south side of the Mohawk; it arrogates to itself being the capital of the Western district. Twenty-two years ago there was but one house; there are now three hundred, a Presbyterian Church, an Episcopal, a Welch Presbyterian, and a Welch Baptist; a Bank, being a branch of the Manhattan Company, a Post Office, the office of the Clerk of the County, and the Clerk of the Supreme Court. By the census now taking, it contains 1,650 inhabitants. Two newspapers are printed here.

The situation of the place is on low ground, a great part of which is natural meadow. It derives its importance from its situation on the Mohawk, the Seneca turnpike which communicates with the heart of the Western country, and the Mohawk and Schenectady turnpike, which leads to Schenectady on the north side of the Mohawk, independently of a good free road on the south side.

Produce is carried by land from Utica to Albany for 8s. per 100 lbs.; by water to Schenectady, for 6s. When the Canal Company reduced the toll, the wagoners reduced their price in order to compete with the competition. Country people owe merchants, and pay their debts by conveyances of this kind, and in times when their teams are not much wanted for other purposes.

Utica bears every external indication of prosperity. Some of the houses are uncommonly elegant; the stores are numerous and well replenished with merchandise. The price of building lots is extravagantly high. Lots, correspondent to double lots in New York, sell here from four to eight hundred dollars. The Bleecker family own 1200 acres in the village and its vicinity, and by at first refusing to sell, and by leasing out at extravagant rates, they greatly injured the growth of the place. They seem now to have embraced a more liberal policy. They have made a turnpike of two miles, and a bridge over the Mohawk, to carry the traveling through their estate; and they have opened streets for sale. They recently sold 2½ acres at auction, for $9,000. The land was divided into 25 lots, fifty by one hundred feet. Judge Cooper of this place bought, about ten years ago, 15 acres for $1,500, which would now sell for $20,000.

The capital of the Manhattan Bank is $100,000. The building is improperly situated close by stables, and is much exposed to fire. In consequence of the trade with Canada, specie is continually accumulating here. It affords a great facility for the transmission of money to and from New York. A small Bank in Connecticut, named the Bridgeport Bank, of which Doctor Bronson is President, discounts notes here through a private agent. Having made an arrangement with the Merchants' Bank of New York, to take its notes, they became in good credit, and had an extensive circulation. As the Branch did not receive their notes in payment, they were constantly accumulating a balance against the institution. With a view to meet this evil, and to turn the tables on the adversary institution, the Branch now take the Bridgeport notes. I found that it is projected by the Directors to increase the stock of the Bank to $500,000; to distribute it in the village, and to maintain its dependence upon, and connection with, the Manhattan Company, in order to prevent it from becoming a federal institution.

The town of Whitestown contains, besides Utica, two considerable villages, West Hartford and Whitesborough. This district of country has twenty-two lawyers.

I met here Bishop Moore, on a diocesan visitation to confirm the members of his Church. Also, Col. Curtenius. Dined at Mr. Kip's, who lives in handsome style, and who received us with great hospitality.

July 11th. Morris and Van Rensselaer were to travel by land as before; here we met Gen. North and the Surveyor. We proceeded by land to Whitesborough, four miles from Utica, and there we divided, some of the company continuing to go by land and others taking to the boats.

Two miles from Utica we visited a famous cheesemaker, named Abraham Bradbury, an English Quaker. He has rented a farm of 163 acres, for $500 per annum. He keeps thirty-six cows, and makes upwards of 400 cheeses a year. Besides the cheese, the milk will support a great number of hogs. He is assisted by his wife and two sisters. His cheese is equal to the best English cheese that is imported, and he vends it for 1s. 3d. per pound. Notwithstanding his high rent, he clears upwards of $1000 a-year by his establishment.

On Sauquoit Creek, a mile from Whitesborough, there is a large manufacturing establishment for spinning cotton. The works go by water. It is owned by a Company, and is denominated the Oneida Manufacturing Society. The stock is said to be profitable, and to be forty per cent above par. It employs forty hands, chiefly young girls, who have an unhealthy appearance. It is on Arkwright's plan, and contains 384 spindles on six frames.

Whitesborough contains the Court-House, and is a handsome village. Several lawyers reside here on account of the Court-House. The federal candidate for governor, Jonas Platt, has a handsome house. Eight miles from Utica we passed Oriskany, where Herkimer's battle was fought.

We arrived at Rome for dinner, and put up at Isaac Lee's house, which is a large double three-story frame building, called the Hotel. He rents it and ten acres of land from Dominick Lynch, for $250 a-year.

Rome is on the highest land between Lake Ontario and the Hudson, at Troy. It is 390 feet above the latter; sixteen miles by land and twenty-one by water from Utica, and 106 miles by water from Schenectady. It is situated at the head of the Mohawk River and Wood Creek, that river running east and the Wood Creek west. You see no hills or mountains in its vicinity; a plain extends from it on all sides. It has a Court-House, a State Arsenal, a Presbyterian Church, and about seventy houses. Its excellent position on the Canal, which unites the Eastern and Western waters, and its natural communication with the rich counties on Black River, would render it a place of great importance, superior to Utica, if fair play had been given to its advantages. But its rising prosperity has been checked by the policy of its principal proprietor [Dominick Lynch]. When he first began to dispose of his lots, he asked what he called a fine of £30, and an annual rent of £7 10s., for each lot forever. His subsequent conduct has been correspondent with this unfavorable indication, and has given Utica a start which Rome can never retrieve.

Two lots, sixty-six by 200 feet, sell from $200 to $250. Wild land in the vicinity sells from $10 to $12 50 per acre, and improved land for $25. A Company was incorporated the last session of the Legislature, for manufacturing iron and glass, and half the stock is already filled up. The place has a Post Office and four lawyers. Rome being on a perfect level, we naturally ask from what has it derived its name. Where are its seven hills? Has it been named out of compliment to Lynch, who is a Roman Catholic?

Rome was laid out into a town, after the Canal was made or contemplated. It derives its principal advantages from this communication. Independent of the general rise it has given to Lynch's property, it has drained a large swamp for him near the village, which would otherwise have been useless; and yet he demanded from the Company, at first, $7,000, and at last, $5,000 for his land, through which the Canal was to pass. The appraisers gave him but nominal damages - one dollar.

The Canal at Rome is 1¾ miles long; 32 feet wide at top, and from 2½ to 3 feet deep. The locks are 73 feet long and 12 wide; 10 feet lift on the Mohawk, and 8 feet on Wood Creek.

July 12th. The Commissioners had a meeting here; all present. Adjourned to meet in Geneva. At this meeting the Senior Commissioner was for breaking down the mound of Lake Erie, and letting out the waters to follow the level of the country, so as to form a sloop navigation with the Hudson, and without any aid from any other water.

The site of Fort Stanwix is in this village. It contains about two acres, and is a regular fortification, with four bastions and a deep ditch. The position is important in protecting the passage between the lakes and the Mohawk river. It is now in ruins, and partly demolished by Lynch, its proprietor. Since the Revolutionary War a block-house was erected here by the State, and is now demolished. About half a mile below the Fort, on the meadows, are the remains of an old fort, called Fort William; and about a mile west of Rome, near where Wood Creek enters the Canal, there was a regular fort, called Fort Newport. Wood Creek is here so narrow that you can step over it.

Fort Stanwix is celebrated in the history of the Revolutionary War, for a regular siege which it stood. And as this and the battle of Oriskany are talked of all over the country, and are not embodied at large in history.

After having dined on a salmon caught at Fish Creek, about eight miles from Rome, we departed in our boats on the descending waters of Wood Creek. And as we have now got rid of the Eastern waters, it may be proper to make some remarks on the Mohawk River.

This river is about 120 miles in length, from Rome to the Hudson. Its course is from west to east. The commencement of its navigation is at Schenectady. It is in all places sufficiently wide for sloop navigation; but the various shoals, currents, rifts, and rapids with which it abounds, and which are very perspicuously laid down on Wright's map, render the navigation difficult even for batteaux. The Canal Company have endeavored, by dams and other expedients, to deepen the river and improve the navigation, but they have only encountered unnecessary expense; the next freshet or rise of the river has either swept away their erections or changed the current. Mr. Weston, the engineer, from a view of the multifarious difficulties attendant on such operations, proposed to make a canal from Schoharie Creek to Schenectady, on the south side of the river; he only erred in not embracing the whole route of the Mohawk. The valley formed by that river is admirably calculated for a canal. The expense of digging it will not exceed that of a good turnpike. The river is good only as a feeder.

The young willows which line the banks of the river, and which are the first trees that spring up on alluviums, show the continual change of ground. No land can be more fertile than the flats of this extensive valley. The settlements here were originally made by migrations from Holland and Germany. The grants under the Dutch Governor were from given points on the Mohawk, embracing all the land south or north, meaning thereby to include only the interval land, and deeming the upland as nothing. Chief-Justice Yates said, that he recollected a witness to state in Court that he had travelled from Kinderhook to Albany and found no land.

The Mohawk is barren of fish. It formerly contained great plenty of trout - it now has none. The largest fish is the pike, which have been caught weighing fourteen pounds. Since the canal at Rome, chubb, a species of dace, have come into the Mohawk through Wood Creek, and are said to be plenty. A salmon and black bass have also been speared in this river, which came into it through the canal. It would not be a little singular if the Hudson should be supplied with salmon through that channel. The falls of the Cohoes oppose a great impediment to the passage of fish; but the Hudson is like the Mohawk, a very sterile river in that respect.

We saw great numbers of bitterns, blackbirds, robins, and bank swallows, which perforate the banks of the river. Also, some wood-ducks, gulls, sheldrakes, bob-linklin, king-birds, crows, kildares, small snipe, woodpeckers, woodcock, wrens, yellow birds, phebes; blue jays, high-holes, pigeons, thrushes, and larks. We also saw several king-fishers, which denote the presence of fish. We shot several bitterns, the same as found on the salt marsh. The only shell fish were the snapping turtle and muscle.

We left Rome after dinner - five Commissioners, the surveyor, and a young gentleman. Morris and Van Rensselaer were to go by land and meet us at Geneva.

We went this day as far as Gilbert's Tavern on the north side of the creek, six and a half miles by water, and four and a half miles by land, from Rome.

We saw a bright red-bird about the size of a blue-bird, Its wings were tipped with black, and the bird uncommonly beautiful. It appeared to have no song, and no one present seemed to know its name. I saw but three besides in the whole course of my tour, one on the Ridge Road west of the Genesee River. It is, therefore, a rara avis.

On the banks of the creek were plenty of boneset, the Canada shrub, said to be useful in medicine, and a great variety of beautiful flowering plants. Wild gooseberry bushes, wild currants, and wild hops were also to be seen. The gooseberries were not good; the hops are said to be as good as the domestic ones. In the long weeds and thick underwood we were at first apprehensive of rattlesnakes, of which we were told there are three kinds - the large and the small, and the dark rattlesnake. But neither here nor in any part of our tour did we see this venomous reptile. The only animals we saw on this stream were the black squirrel and the hare, as it is called in Albany, a creature white in winter, of the rabbit kind, although much larger.

About a mile from the head of the creek we passed a small stream, from the south, called Black or Mud Creek. Above Gilbert's the Company have erected four wooden locks, which are absolutely necessary, at a small expense, when compared with their stone locks at the Little Falls, which cost $500. The Com-

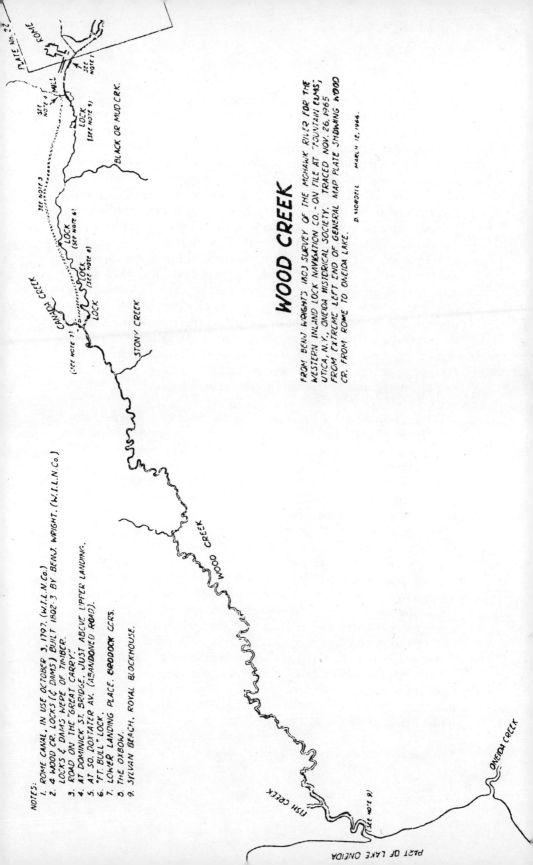

WOOD CREEK

FROM BENJ WRIGHT'S 1803 SURVEY OF THE MOHAWK RIVER FOR THE WESTERN INLAND LOCK NAVIGATION CO.- ON FILE AT "FOUNTAIN ELMS", UTICA, N.Y., ONEIDA HISTORICAL SOCIETY. TRACED NOV. 26, 1965 FROM EXTREME LEFT END OF GENERAL MAP PLATE SHOWING WOOD CR. FROM ROME TO ONEIDA LAKE.   D. SKORDELL   MARCH 12, 1966.

NOTES:
1. ROME CANAL, IN USE OCTOBER 3, 1797. (W.I.L.N.Co.)
2. 4 WOOD CR. LOCKS (¿ DAMS) BUILT 1802-3 BY BENJ. WRIGHT. (W.I.L.N.Co.)
   LOCKS ¿ DAMS WERE OF TIMBER.
3. ROAD ON THE "GREAT CARRY."
4. AT DOMINICK ST. BRIDGE. JUST ABOVE (UPPER LANDING.
5. AT SO. DOXTATER AV. (ABANDONED ROAD).
6. "FT. BULL" LOCK.
7. LOWER LANDING PLACE. BRODOCK CCRS.
8. THE OXBOW.
9. SYLVAN BEACH. ROYAL BLOCKHOUSE.

PLATE No. 22

ROME

MILL

SEE NOTE 1

SEE NOTES 4 & 5

LOCK (SEE NOTE 2)

BLACK OR MUD CRK.

SEE NOTE 3

CANADA CREEK

LOCK (SEE NOTE 6)

LOCK (SEE NOTE 2)

LOCK (SEE NOTE 2)

(SEE NOTE 7)

STONY CREEK

WOOD CREEK

FISH CREEK

(SEE NOTE 9)

ONEIDA CREEK

PART OF LAKE ONEIDA

pany have also shortened the distance on the whole route of the creek about four miles, the whole distance being about 28 miles, by cutting canals to meet the serpentine bend of the stream. It is susceptible of being shortened, so as to make only sixteen miles. The State reserved a thousand acres of the south side, from Gilbert's down to the Oneida Lake, to be applied to the improvement of the navigation. This land is overrun by squatters. From some causes which cannot be satisfactorily explained, unless connected with our mission, the stock of this Company can now be bought for $200 a share - the nominal value is $250.

We passed, on the north side of the creek, the appearance of an old fortification, called Fort Bull. The remains of an old dam, to impede the passage of a hostile fleet, and to assist the operations of the fort, were also to be seen. Although there is now a road on that side of the creek, yet in those days there could have been no marching by land with an army. The transportation of provisions must have been impracticable by land; and, indeed, the general appearance of the country exhibits a sunken morass or swamp, overgrown with timber and formed from the retreat of the lake.

Gilbert's house is a decent comfortable house, considering the little resort of travelers. The grounds around it are overflown by the creek, and the situation unhealthy. He had procured fresh salmon from Fish creek for us, at 6d. a lb. We found it excellent. In the neighborhood of Gilbert's there is said to be good bog ore;* we saw specimens furnished by a man who had come to explore the country for that purpose.

We rose early in the morning, and breakfasted at the Oak-Orchard, six miles from Gilbert's on the south side of the river. The ground was miry, and in stepping in the boat, my foot slipped, and I was partly immersed in the creek. The captain assisted me in getting out. The dampness of the weather, and the sun being hardly risen, induced me, for greater precaution, to change my clothes. This trifling incident was afterwards magnified by the papers into a serious affair.

Near Gilbert's, the Canada Creek comes in from the north side, a mile west the Rocky or Black Creek, from the south. At Oak-Orchard the first rapid commences; as the creek was extremely low, we requested that locks to be left open above, two or three hours before we started. This furnished us with a flood of water,

* Not bog ore (limonite), but fossil and oolitic hematite.

and accelerated our descent. We found, however, that we went faster than the water, and had frequently to wait. The creek was almost the whole distance choked with logs, and crooked beyond belief; in some places after bending in the most serpentine direction for a mile, it would return just below the point of departure. From Wright's survey, the distance-

	Miles
From Gilbert's to the mouth of the creek, by the old route - is	21
By the present route, as improved by the Canal Company, ...	17
On a straight line, which is practicable for a Canal, ...	9

We stopped at Smith's, a German, who lives on the south side of the creek, and about eight miles from the Oneida Lake. The creek is sandy, and very winding from this place, - the sand, accumulated at such a distance from the lake, demonstrates the truth of my theory respecting the formation of the ground from Rome to the lake. Smith is not forty years of age, and has been settled here fifteen years. He has six daughters, five of whom are married; two sons, twenty-five grand-children, and one great-grand-child, who almost all reside in his vicinity. The female part of his descendants were assembled to rake his hay; their children were brought with them, and the whole exhibited a picture of rural manners and rude industry, not unpleasing.

About six miles from the lake we saw the remains of a batteaux, sunk by the British on their retreat from the siege of Fort Stanwix.

Four miles from the lake we dined at one Babbits', on the north side of the creek. We found, on such occasions, our own provisions and liquors, and were only provided with house-room and fire for cooking. The family were obliging and simple. They had been forewarned of our approach, and their attention was turned towards the contemplated canal. As they are the proprietors of the soil, which was purchased from General [Alexander] Hamilton, they were apprehensive that the canal would be diverted from them, and pass through Camden, and the old lady said she would charge us nothing, if we straitened the creek and lowered the lake. The only potable water here is from the creek, which is very bad, and no other can be procured, as the creek is on a level with the surrounding country. The family furnished us with tolerable vinegar, made of maple juice. The old lady, on being interrogated as to the religion she professed, said that she belonged to the church, but what church she could not tell. The oracle of the family was a deformed, hump-backed young man called John. On all occasions his opinions were as decisive as the responses of the sybil; and he reminded us of the Arabian Night's Entertainment, which represents persons hump-backed as possessed of great shrewdness. John told us a story of Irish Peggy, a girl whom he described as going down in a batteaux, so handsome and well-dressed that she attracted him and all the young men in the neighborhood, who visited the charming creature; that on her return some weeks afterwards, she looked as ugly as she had been before beautiful, and was addicted to swearing and drunkenness; that she had been indirectly the cause of the death of three men; that one of them, a negro, was drowned in a lock, who had gone to sleep on the deck of the boat, in order to accommodate her and her paramour; that another fell overboard, when she had retired with her gallant, and prevented by it assistance that might have saved him; and that the third one experienced a similar fate. The commodore did not fail to extract a moral from John's story, favorable to the cause of good morals; and admonished him to beware to the lewd woman, "whose house is the way to hell, going down to the chambers of death."

A boat passed us at this house, which speared a salmon with a boat-hook in passing under a bridge. The frequent passage of boats, and the shallowness of the waters, terrify the salmon from ascending in great numbers beyond this place.

We passed James Dean's old house on the right, about two miles from the lake. He first went among the Oneidas as a silversmith, vending trinkets. He afterwards acted as an interpreter, and coaxed them out of large tracts of land. He is now rich, a Judge of Oneida county, has been a member of Assembly, and is a prominent Federalist.

Fish Creek enters Wood Creek, a mile from the lake, on the north side. It is much larger and deeper, and derives its name from the excellent fish with which it abounds, up to the Falls, which are ten miles from its mouth. It is frequented by great numbers of salmon; and we saw Indians with their spears at work after that fish, and met two canoes going on the same business, with their pine knots and apparatus ready for the attack. The Indians have reserved the land on each side of this creek, in order to secure themselves the benefit of fishing.

The confluence of these streams makes a considerable river

from this place to the Oneida Lake, deep, wide, and gloomy, and resembling the fabled Avernus. You can see the track of its black and muddy waters a considerable distance in the great basin into which it discharges.

We arrived at Mrs. Jackson's tavern, at seven o'clock, near the mouth of Wood Creek, which enters Oneida Lake from the north-east. To the west, the eye was lost in the expanse of waters, there being no limits to the horizon. A western wind gently agitated the surface of the waters. A number of canoes darting through the lake after fish in a dark night, with lighted flambeaux of pine knots fixed on elevated iron frames, made a very picturesque and pleasing exhibition. We walked on the beach, composed of the finest sand, like the shores of the ocean, and covered with a few straggling trees. Here we met with an Indian canoe, filled with eels, salmon, and monstrous cat-fish. In another place we saw the native of the woods cooking his fish and eating his meal on the beach. We could not resist the temptation of the cold bath. On returning to the house, we found an excellent supper prepared; the principal dish was salmon, dressed in various ways.

The salmon come into this lake in May, and continue till winter. They are said to eat nothing. This is the season of their excellence. They formerly sold for one shilling a-piece; now the current price is sixpence a pound. The salmon are annoyed by an insect called a tick, and run up into the cold spring brooks for relief.

Near this tavern there are to be seen the marks of an old fortification, covering about one-eighth of an acre, and called the Royal Block-House. In this place, Col. Porter and the young gentlemen made a tent of the sails and setting poles, and, with the aid of a fire and our mattresses, had a good night's lodging. The other Commissioners slept in the house; the window panes were out and the doors open. The resort of Indians and the sandy ground had drawn together a crowd of fleas, which, with the mosquitoes, annoyed us beyond sufferance the whole night. Some of the family sat up late; the creakings of a crazy old building and the noise of voices, added to our other annoyances, completely deprived us of rest. The house was in other respects a comfortable one. The ice, which we used to correct the badness of the creek water, had a pleasant effect.

We found here a new species of mullen, with a white bushy top of flowers. Sometimes the top was yellow. The common mullen

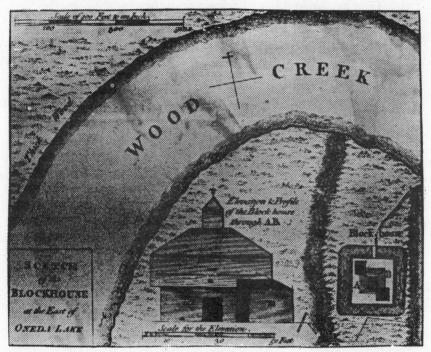

Rome Historical Society

Royal Blockhouse at entrance of Wood Creek

was also plenty.

July 14th. Although the wind on this lake is generally easterly in the morning and westerly in the afternoon, yet we had no other resource than our oars. At the entrance of the Wood Creek, and about fifty rods from its mouth, we found a sand-bar forty rods wide. The shallowest part was two feet deep, and the channel between three and four feet wide.

The Oneida Creek comes in on the south side of the lake. At its mouth it is about as large as Wood Creek, and as you ascend one-third larger. There are no bars at its mouth. The salmon go up as far as Stockbridge. This Creek, Wood Creek, and Canaseragas Creek, are the principal sources which supply the Oneida Lake. According to the general computation, this lake is thirty miles long, but it does not exceed twenty miles in length, and from five to eight in breath. In winter it freezes, and is passable in sleighs.

The waters of the lake are saturated with small dark atoms, which render them unsalubrious, and when drank, operate emetically, and produce fever. This, in the language of the boatmen, is termed the lake blossom. Whether it arises from the farina of the chestnut, or any other trees that blossom about this time, the eggs of insects, or collections of animalculae, we could not determine. We examined the water by a microscope, and could come to no conclusion. If I were to give an opinion, it would be, that it is not an animal substance, but small atoms swept into the lake by the waters of Wood Creek, from the vegetable putrefactions generated in the swamps and marshes through which that stream runs.

Independently of several collections of sand and reeds, which can hardly be termed islands, and of an islet about the middle of the lake, which has a single tree, and looks at a distance like a ship under sail, there are two islands, about two miles from the outlet, half a mile from the south shore of the lake. They are within a short distance from each other. One island contains fourteen acres, and the other, called Frenchman's Island, twenty-seven acres. A person can wade from one to the other; and bears, in swimming the lake, frequently stop here to rest. These islands belong to the State.

One of the islands is called the Frenchman's Island, from a person of that nation, who took possession of it about fifteen years ago, with a beautiful wife. He resided there until the cold weather came, and then he wintered in Albany, Rome, or Rotterdam. He had a handsome collection of books, musical instruments, and all the appendages of former opulence and refinement. He was apparently discontented and depressed - cultivated a handsome garden with his own hands, and sowed half-an-acre of wheat, which had a beautiful appearance. His wife bore him children here, and altogether he had three. He became by practice a very expert fowler, hunter, and angler, and was a hard worker. He lived here seven summers. He spent a winter at the Oneida Castle, and sent his clothes for washing sometimes to Albany. When he first came, he had a considerable sum of money, and, becoming poor, he sold some of his books for subsistence, and he bartered some valuable ones to Major Dezeng for two cows. He was very proud and reserved - went at last bare headed [deranged], and the general suspicion was, that jealousy was the cause of his seclusion. They visited their neighbor Stevens, at the outlet, twice a year. We were told by Mrs. Stevens, that his name was Devity or Devitzy; that his countrymen in Albany made a subscription, which enabled him to go to France, with his family; that she returned the visits of the family, and found them apparently happy; and that in her opinion, the Frenchwoman had no extraordinary pretensions to beauty.

We stopped at a house at the north side of the lake, in the town of Bengal [Vienna]. The proprietor bought sixty-six acres from J. Munro, for four dollars an acre. The family were eagerly engaged in the salmon fishing, and they told us that they sometimes caught with the seine one hundred per day; that fifteen fill a large barrel, for which they ask twelve dollars in salt. They also informed us that shad recently came up the lake. The salmon frequently weighs twenty pounds. The black or Oswego bass is a fine fish, sometimes weighing eight pounds, and is like our black fish, but harder.

The Commission on its return trip to Albany reached Lenox, Madison County on the 16th of August.

Slept at Stockton's last night, and breakfasted there this morning. We found it the best tavern on the road. He lives in Lenox, Madison County, and migrated from Princeton, New Jersey. He is styled Doctor. He lives on the borders of the Oneida Reservation, twenty-five miles from Utica, and fourteen miles from Lake Oneida. Opposite to him is the settlement of the Oneida Indians called the Squalone village; and a little west is the Squalone Creek, a handsome stream, which empties in the Canaseraga.

We found the morning chilly, although we set out after seven. The change of climate from the Onondaga Hills is very perceptible. I experienced this kind of weather last summer at Cherry Valley.

The Seneca turnpike passes through the Oneida Reservation, which is five miles from east to west. Oneida Creek is a fine stream, about eight miles from Oneida Lake. Salmon run up it eight miles higher, as far as Stockbridge. At the end of the bridge over it there stood a beautiful Indian girl, offering apples for sale to the persons that passed. The Missionary church, in which Mr. Kirkland formerly preached, and an Indian schoolhouse, are here. We saw Indian boys trying to kill birds; others driving cattle over plains. Some Indians plowing with oxen, and at the same time their heads ornamented with white feathers; some driving a wagon, and the women milking and churning, - all the indications of incipient civilization.

About four miles from Stockton's we stopped at Skenando's house. He was formerly the Chief Sachem of all the Oneidas; but since the nation has been split up into Christian and Pagan parties, he is only acknowledged by the former. The Chief of the latter is Capt. Peter, a very sensible man. The morals of the Pagans are better than those of the Christians. The former still practice some of their ancient superstitions. On the first new moon of every new year, they sacrifice a white dog to the Great Spirit, and devote six days to celebrate the commencement of the year. The Christian party are more numerous, by one hundred, than the Pagan. They are entirely separated in their territory, as well as in their God.

Skenando is one hundred and one years old, and his wife is seventy-four. He is weak, and can hardly walk. His face is good and benevolent, and not much wrinkles. He is entirely blind; but his hair is not gray. He smokes; and can converse a little in English. He was highly delighted with an elegant silver pipe, that was given to him by Gov. Tompkins. His wife was afflicted with the bronchocele, or goitre. It is like a wen, promulging from the neck, near the thorax. There were some cases near Utica some years ago. A number of his children and grandchildren were present. His daughter looked so old that first I took her for his wife. Some of the females were handsome. His house is one hundred yards from the road, situated on the margin of a valley, through which a pleasant stream flows. It is a small frame building, painted red; and adjoining it is a log house. Before the settlement of the country he kept a tavern, like the first Governor of Vermont, for the accommodation of travellers. There were four bedsteads in the room, composed of coarse wooden bunks, so called, and covered by blankets and pillows, instead of beds. A large kettle of corn was boiling, which was the only breakfast the family appeared to have. It was occasionally dipped out from the pot into a basket, from which the children ate. The furniture and farming utensils were coarse, and those of civilized persons.

His eldest son, Thomas, came in, spruced-up like an Indian beau. The expression of his countenance is very malignant; but his features are handsome. He ate out of the basket. It is said, that on his father's demise, he will succeed him as Chief Sachem; but if I understand their system right, the office of Sachem is personal, and not hereditary. It is said that Skenando is opulent, for an Indian; and that Thomas has frequently attempted to kill him, with a view of enjoying his property; alledging, too, that his father is not liberal, and that he has lived long enough. Such is the mode of living of the first Chief of an Indian nation. In England he would be recognized as a king - as were the five Mohawk Chiefs that went there with Col. Schuyler, in the reign of Queen Anne, and who are mentioned in the Spectator.

Abraham Hatfield and his wife (Quakers), have resided here sometime; having been sent by that Society principally with a view to teach the savages agriculture; for which they receive $200 a year. Hatfield was sick; his wife appeared to be a kind, good woman; well qualified for the duties allotted to her. They are amply provided with oxen and the instruments of agriculture, to administer to the wants and instruction of the Indians. The Oneida's are much attached to the Quakers. They teach morals - not dogmas - agriculture, and the arts of civilized life. Those of England have divided £8,000 among the Friends of Baltimore, Philadelphia, and New York, in order to ameliorate the condition of the Indians. The means adopted by the Quakers are the only competent ones that can be adopted. They indicate a knowledge of human nature; and if the Indians are ever rescued effectually from the evils of savage life, it will be through their instrumentality. The Missionary Societies have been of little use in this nation. The morals of the Christians are worse than those of the Pagans. The clergyman at Stockbridge, of the name of Sergeant, notwithstanding the goodness of his intentions, has not been able to effect much.

In this village we observed several very old Indian women; and there was an old Indian, named the Blacksmith, recently dead, older than Skenando, who used to say that he was at a treaty with William Penn. There was a boy far gone in a consumption - which was a prevalent disease among them. Last winter they were severely pressed by famine; and, admonished by experience, they intend to put in considerable wheat - to which they have hitherto been opposed - and they now have large crops of corn. They appear to be well provided with neat cattle and hogs. Some of the Indians are very squalid and filthy. I saw several take lice from their heads. They evince great parental fondness, and are much pleased with any attention to their children. An Indian child in Skenando's house took hold of my cane: to divert him I gave him some small money; the mother appeared much pleased, and immediately offered me apples to eat - the best thing she had to give.

In passing the Oneida Reservation we saw some white settlers, and it is not a little surprising that they receive any encouragement from the Indians, considering how often they have been coaxed out of their lands by their white brethren. I shall give a few prominent illustrations.

1. Peter Smith, a former clerk of Abraham Herring - he established a store in their country - called a son Skenando, after their Chief, and by wheedling the Legislature as well as the Indians, he has succeeded in acquiring an immense body of excellent land at a low price, and he is now very opulent.

2. Michael Wemple, a Dutch blacksmith, sent among them by Gen. Washington.

3. James Dean, formerly a toy-maker, interpreter among them.

4. The Rev. Mr. Kirkland, missionary and interpreter.

Lastly, Angel De Ferriere. He left France in the time of Robespiere. His mother is rich, and has written for him to return to his country; but he declines on account, as he says, of his red wife. He first lived with Mr. Lincklaen, at Cazenovia; and at sometimes exhibited symptoms of mental derangement. He then went to reside among the Oneidas, and married the daughter of Louis Dennie, before-mentioned, by a squaw - a well-behaved woman of civilized manners and habits, and resembling an Indian in nothing but color. He has by her three children. He has been among the Indians twelve years. Being a man of genteel manners, sensible, and well-informed, he acquired a great influence over them, and has prevailed on them to confer on him donations of valuable land - which have been sanctioned by the State. At the last session, the Christian party sold for $3,050.02 and an annuity, a part of their Reservation, and in the treaty made with them they appropriated ____ acres for De Ferriere. He owns 1700 acres of the best land - a great deal of it on the turnpike - the tavern occupied by Dr. Stockton, a large two-story house, grist mill and saw mill on the creek, and distillery, and is supposed to be worth $50,000. He lives in a loghouse about a half mile from Stockton's; and, I am told, is always involved in law suits. At present, he has no more particular intercourse with the Indians than any other white in their vicinity. His father-in-law, Louis Dennie, is quite proud of his opulent son-in-law. He is a savage in all respects; and says it is hard times with the Indians; the game is all gone - that he recollects that deer were as thick as leaves in Schoharie before it was settled. That country belonged to the Mohawks. John Dennie, before-mentioned, was Louis's son. His wife addicted to intemperance, and their children are said to be the worst-tempered of any in the nation.

August 16th, 1810, continued.   After the Oneida Reservation we entered the town of Vernon, in which three glass-houses are in contemplation; one has been in operation some time. It is rather to be regretted that this business is overdone. Besides the glass introduced from Pittsburgh, and from a glass-house in Pennsylvania, on the borders of Orange county, and the glass imported from Europe, there are ten manufactories in the State already, or about to be established - one in Guilderland, Albany county; one in Rensselaer county; three in Vernon, Oneida county; one in Utica, do.; one in Rome, do.; one in Peterborough, Madison county; one in Geneva, Ontario county; one in Woodstock, Ulster county.

The village of Mount Vernon is eight miles from Stockton's. It is by a fine creek and celebrated mills of that name, and has a Post-office, several stores, and about twenty houses.

We passed on the road Elias Hicks, a Quaker preacher, Isaac Hicks and another Friend, Mrs. Haydock and another female Friend, on a mission from a yearly meeting of New York, to open a half-yearly meeting in York, Upper Canada.

We dined at Noah Leavins' tavern, in Westmoreland, twelve miles from Utica. He gave for this house and a farm of 150 acres, last May, $5,000. His house is well kept; but he says he is determined to make it among the best on the road. We advised him to buy a demijohn of the best Madeira wine, $25; two dozen claret,

$20; a cask of porter, $15; and half a box of segars, $9; and to have these for select guests, who understood their value, and that his house would soon acquire a great name. That he ought to have his house painted; to establish an icehouse, and to be very particular in having good and clean beds; for that after all a traveler was perhaps more solicitous about good lodging than anything else. His wife, although from Connecticut, in dress looks like and appears to be a Dutchwoman. This shows the power of imitation; she resided in a Dutch village for some time.

The country out of the Oneida Reservation to this place is fertile, no bad land, and well settled; the road good, and as populous as a village.

About a mile from Leavins' we passed a church; a plain framed building, not painted. We saw in some places men pounding limestone, with which to imbed the turnpike, and part of the way this has already been accomplished, and resembles the road between Bristol and Philadelphia. This great turnpike, from Canandaigua to Utica, is the vital principle of the latter place, and yet it has been so recently made, that in some places you can perceive the remains of stumps. Nine miles from Utica we passed the Oriskany Creek, a considerable stream. Six or seven miles from Utica, there is a string of houses extending a considerable distance, forming a village called the Middle Settlement. Three or four miles from Utica is New Hartford, a flourishing and prosperous village; a fine stream runs by it, on which are mills, and it contains a Presbyterian church. As you pass to the east end of the village, and look up the valley to the south, you behold a delightful, populous country.

In reflecting on Louis Dennie's information about the Spanish Expedition, two reflections occurred: -

Are there any Indian Forts north of Oswego, or east of Manlius, or generally speaking out of the line designated by him?

May not the Spaniards have come into Canada, and so on to Oswego, by the way of the Mississippi, up the Fox or Illinois River, and returned by the Ohio, independently of the usual route by the St. Lawrence?

We passed a school taught by a young woman; this is a common practice in the western country.

August 17th. Utica.   The day being rainy we spent it at Utica; we put up at Bellinger's inn, but I staid at James S. Kip's, Esq., who has a very large elegant stone house, that cost $9,000. I saw at his house Walter Bowne, on his way to Niagara; Mr. Hunt, the cashier of the bank; Mr. Arthur Breese, Mr. Bloodgood, Mr. Walker, the printer, Dr. Wolcott, Judge Cooper, and several others. And this day Mr. Kip had to dinner, besides our company, Walker, Breese, Bloodgood, and Brodhead. The report of the quarrel between Jackson and Morris had reached this place much exaggerated; and my slipping into Wood Creek, was represented as a hair-breadth escape. The death of the Lieutenant-Governor was confirmed here: this worthy man took his final departure on the eighth of August, in the fullness of years and honor. He had just engaged his quarters at Albany for the ensuing legislative campaign.

A map of the northern part of this State was published in 1801, by Amos Lay and Arthur J. Stansbury, and said to be compiled from actual survey.

Botany is cultivated in the Western District. A man at Palmyra has established a garden, in which he cultivates poppy, palma Christi, and a number of our native plants.

It is not perhaps too exaggerated to say, that the worst lands in the western country are nearly equal to the best in the Atlantic parts of the State. There appears to be a great deal of alluvial land in the former.

Ashes boiled down in order to be portable, are termed black salts, and are purchased by the country merchants, in order to manufacture into potash.

I amused myself today in reading a curious speech, delivered before a proposed Agricultural Society in Whitestown, and published in 1795, by F. Adrian Vanderkemp, an emigrant from Holland, abounding with bad style, but containing some good ideas. He proposes premiums for certain dissertations, and among others, "for the best anatomical or historical account of the moose $50, or for bringing one in alive $60." The moose now exists in the northern parts of the State, as does the elk in the southern.

Dr. Wolcott, the Post-master at Utica, says that out of twelve cases of Spotted fever which came under his cognizance, he has cured eleven by the speedy application of tonics, such as bark and wine; that he considers it a disease rising from specific contagion, and operating by a dissolution of the fluids.

Seneca River is the best for navigation; Oneida the next; Wood Creek the next, and the Mohawk the worst. A canal can be made along the valley of the latter for $2,000 a mile.

Mr. Kip has a pump which works with amazing facility; the

handle is iron, and goes by a lever on the side, instead of the center of the pump. It would be very useful in New York.

Whiskey manufactured from grain, is the purest spirit drank in this country, and when strained through charcoal is freed from empyreumatic oil.

I met Joe Winter here, who is styled Judge Winter when over the brandy bottle with his low companions. He told me that he owns a farm at Springfield, in Otsego county, worth $4,000; that he brought an action of trespass by Seeley, an attorney of Cherry Valley, and was disposed, owing to his negligence; and that this farm is advertised to be sold for the costs, on Monday next, which cannot exceed $20; that he has had no notice of it from the Sheriff, with whom he is intimate, or his attorney; and that in all probability the property would have been designedly sacrificed, if it had not been for the zeal of a friend, who gave him notice at Utica.

Part of the capital of Boston has been transferred to Montreal, and particularly two rich commercial houses. Last year 1300 barrels of potash were sent by three merchants from Black River to Utica. This year not one - it has all gone to Montreal.

August 18th. We left Utica at six o'clock, in a coachee and baggage wagon, for which we were to pay $50 to Albany, and breakfasted at Maynard's tavern, an excellent house, fifteen miles from Utica, in the village of Herkimer.

NOTICES

OF

MEN AND EVENTS

CONNECTED WITH THE

EARLY HISTORY OF ONEIDA COUNTY.

TWO LECTURES, DELIVERED BEFORE THE YOUNG MENS' ASSOCIATION

OF THE CITY OF UTICA,

BY WILLIAM TRACY

Published at the request of the Association.

UTICA:

R. NORTHWAY, Jr. PRINTER, 116 GENESEE STREET.

1838.

LECTURE I.

About seventy-three years since, a youth who had just completed his academical career, and had been inducted into the sacred office of a christian teacher, met at a social interview in a small town in New Jersey, a middle aged minister of the gospel, and a venerable saint, whose name will live when ages shall have rolled away, and be reverenced while piety exists on earth. The youth, full of zeal in the service he had espoused, was seeking a theatre wherein to proclaim the glad tidings of salvation by the Cross, and the fullness and freeness of divine grace. He had sought the advice of these friends, to direct him where to go to do the will of his Master, and best obey the parting injunction of his Lord. The middle-aged minister told him, that in early life, as the chaplain of a regiment of the colonial troops, who in the war between France and the British American colonies, had been ordered to the wilderness which lay westward from the German settlements on the Mohawk, to the great lakes, he had traversed the country of the warlike but noble nations of the Iroquois. For a time he had sojourned in the neighborhood of the Oneidas, and had tasted of their hospitality, and become acquainted with their habits and manner of life. He portrayed them as the noblest of the sons of the forest. Fierce and untiring in warfare, but generous, hospitable, grateful and benevolent in their domestic life. As the worshippers of the one Great Spirit of all good; but ignorant of the attributes which he had revealed to the favored sons of civilization, they, like the men of Athens, worshipped an unknown God. He spoke of the country they inhabited, beautiful even in its native wilderness state, and abounding in all that was necessary to render its possessors the most favored sons of earth. And he painted from fancy and with a poet's pencil, the scene it might exhibit, when these sons of the forest, had become enlightened with the true light which shineth from above, and when the arts, and comforts, and elegancies of civilization, with the holy hopes of christianity, had become their portion; - when their country had sprung from the blooming wilderness, to the picturesque and cultivated and ornamented field and grove and garden; its homely wigwam and its rude cabin, to the stately mansion and magnificent hall; - when seminaries of learning, and halls of science, and temples of the Most High, occupied the places where the stillness of the forest only echoed to the yells of wild beasts, or the rude gaiety, or the piercing war cry of its savage lords. And when he had dwelt a moment on the picture, he pointed out the happiness of him, who should go the messenger and apostle of christianity to their land, and aid in accomplishing such a glorious change.

The soul of the youth felt with all its force the eloquence of his friend, and warmed with a new impulse as he figured to himself the scene thus laid before him; and when the venerated Whitfield, for he was the aged servant of the cross I have before mentioned, urged him to go forth to that field of his Lord, and manfully to lay his sickle to that harvest, he gave himself with the determination of a Christian martyr, to the proclaiming to the wild men of that region, the glorious hopes and promises of the gospel. And the history of a long life chequered with many a vicissitude, furnishes ample proof that his youthful vow became the load star of his maturer years. He went forth with the blessing of his aged friend, and the warm wishes of him who had pointed out his path, and who I would here remark was the Rev. Mr. Kirkpatrick, father of the late Doctor Kirkpatrick of Salina, and sought the beautiful land we now inhabit, then untenanted, save by its native lords, to become their friend, their instructor, and their guide to happiness - to Heaven!

This was Samuel Kirkland, the early, the devoted, the beloved friend of the Oneidas: and in attempting to amuse you for an hour with brief notices of men and events connected with the early history of Oneida county, I feel that it is but justice that his name should occupy my foremost page. A native of an obscure parish in Connecticut, to whose inhabitants his father broke the bread of life as a christian pastor, he had early devoted himself to

Gridley History of the Town of Kirkland

Rev. Samuel Kirkland

the christian ministry, and had received the advantages of a classical education at the college at Princeton, N.J. Possessed of native talents which would have enabled him to occupy a distinguished place among the clergymen of the age, and all the adventitious aids which the means of education in this country then afforded, no ambitious views or sordid hope of gain, could have influenced him, in turning his back upon the abodes of civilization, relinquishing all the pleasure of society, and making the wilderness his home, the wild man his companion, and the object of his care. Nor was there at the time he thus resolved to devote himself to the happiness of the native inhabitants of our land, the cordials which now sustain the drooping spirits of the missionary in heathen lands, furnished by the sympathy of friends at home, and the excitement of constant communication with them, by means of published and wide spread reports and a teeming press. Then, the missionary as he entered the forest, felt that a deep night separated him from all the conversation, and the very thoughts of his former friends, and he could only look to the performance of his duties, and the smiles of his heavenly Master, to sustain his spirit in the trials he must endure.

The period at which the Rev. Mr. Kirkland commenced his mission to the Oneidas was the year 1766. Previous to this time no christian teacher had undertaken to learn their language and establish himself among them. They were as I have observed the worshippers of the Great Spirit, - the creator of all things; but were destitute of any rational, or indeed, fixed notions relative to his attributes. He commenced his labors among them, and immediately undertook the task of teaching them, - living among them and endearing himself to them by his attention, and his amiable and sympathizing spirit. Many of them gave a listening ear to his instructions, and the heart of the good man was often gladdened with the encouragement which met his endeavors, as if to cheer him on his course.

The approach of the troubles of the revolution, after a residence of eight or nine years among them rendered it necessary for him to intermit a portion of his strictly ministerial labors. The Six Nations during the whole colonial history of our country had cultivated a firm and warm friendship with the English government, and espoused their cause in the difficulties which had taken place between them and the French colonies in Canada. At the commencement of the hostilities between the colonists and the royal authorities, several of the tribes constituting them, adhered to their former friends, while a portion became the friends and allies of the colonists. Of the former was the whole of the Mohawks, who after the final triumph of the native Americans, removed with their English allies to Canada, where they now reside. Among the Oneidas, a large portion of the nation attached themselves to the revolutionary party, and though maintaining a neutral position, remained during the whole contest for our liberties the firm and consistent friends of the Americans. There were, however, among the Oneidas many who doubted the propriety of making cause with the colonists, and preferred a league with the royal party. Under these circumstances, prudence and duty dictated to the present subject of our notice, the necessity of removing his family from a position likely to become the theatre of intestine war, and he accordingly established it for a season at Stockbridge, Mass., but still in the spirit of his vow, continued his labor as an Indian missionary among the Oneidas, and by his influence with them, contributed very much to the maintenance of a firm friendship between a great majority of the nation and the Americans. During a portion of the war, in addition to his missionary labors, he officiated as chaplain to the American forces in the vicinity, and among other services accompanied the expedition of General Sullivan through the western part of New York in the year 1779 in this capacity. After the peace, the government of this state, in consideration of his valuable services during the revolution, granted to him the lands lying in the town of Kirkland's Patent, upon a portion of which Hamilton College stands. To these lands he removed his family in the year 1792, and continued upon them during the remainder of his life, occupying the homestead near the village of Clinton which still remains the home of his widow.

At this period in the history of the Oneidas, the nation had scarcely been touched with the contaminating influence, which the approach of white settlements has everywhere shed upon the aboriginal inhabitants of our country. As yet, the soil of a greater part of our county belonged to it, and the Indian lad as he pursued the deer over his native hills, could with full truth declare,

"This is my OWN,"-

as well as

"my native land."

Her race of warriors and orators was not yet extinct; and much as has been said of the eloquence of the Indian, I have nowhere met with more touching and purely eloquent specimens of Indian oratory, than those which tradition has preserved us, pronounced by the orators and chiefs of the Oneidas. Most of you will recognize the following introductory passage from one of Sconondoa's addresses to his tribe at a treaty for the sale of their lands: -

"I am an aged hemlock - the winds of an hundred winters have whistled through my tops and withered my branches."

Few more striking or poetical figures are to be found in any language. We can see the aged chief rising to address his countrymen; - the form once erect, and full of health, and strength, and vigor, now bowed down and tottering with the effects of his "hundred winters," and his sightless balls vainly turned towards the sons and grandsons of those with whom his youth and his manhood had been spent. He rises to caution them not to part with the home of their fathers, - the happy playgrounds of generations of their countrymen, and the graves of those who gave them birth; and with trembling voice he utters the words I have just repeated. And as the orator proceeded, and enchained the eyes and the feelings of his whole nation, who could have witnessed the scene, and not curse the hand that should separate from their beloved land, a people so susceptible to the noblest art of all time!

Another of the chiefs of the Oneidas, at the period of which I am now speaking, who is said to have been the equal of Sconondoa in eloquence, was a much younger man, who commonly bore the German soubriquet of Plattcopf. It is said that his influence in the nation was not so great as that of Sconondoa, though he was frequently more forcible in his public addresses. A gentleman who was present at a council, held some years after the revolutionary war, by commissioners on the part of the state to treat for the purchase of a portion of the lands then reserved by the Oneidas, gives an account of a very effective address of this man. The council was held at Oneida, beneath a large pine tree which some of my audience may remember, as once standing on the south side of the turnpike at a short distance beyond the present village, and which tree was some years afterwards struck by lightning. For two days, the warriors of the nation had assembled to consult as to the sale, and as was customary among the Six Nations, the final decision was left to the squaws, who being the cultivators are by a very equitable rule of Indian law regarded as the proprietors of the soil. The whole nation, male and female had now assembled, and the question which was to determine whether it should retain its lands or still further circumscribe its already diminished inheritance was to be settled. Plattcopf arose and addressed the multitude. He spoke of the glory of the nation, previous to the coming of the white man. He said that the Oneidas were then full of strength and vigor and beauty. He pointed to the tree under which they stood, and which although still magnificent for its size and beauty, was visibly marked with age and decay. We were like this tree, said he. It was then young and vigorous and beautiful. It drew its nourishment from the ground - the soil, and it was not cramped and confined; - it could draw nourishment from the whole soil, - for the Oneidas owned it all; - they had parted with none of their possessions. And as the tree could draw sustenance from the whole soil, it grew and put forth more branches, and more leaves, and set out new roots and implanted them deeper in the ground. It became strong and very beautiful: so did the Oneidas. As the tree grew, the white man came, and we sold him a portion of our lands. A root of the tree which depended for its nourishment upon this land withered, for it had no soil; and as it withered a branch died, and the tree lost some of its beauty. Again the white man came, and we sold him another piece of our land; another root withered, and another branch died, and the tree became less beautiful and less vigorous. The white man came a third time, and we sold him another piece of land; - another and another root withered, and another and another branch fell down, and we now see the tree; though beautiful, it has lost its branches, and it no longer sends forth new roots and puts forth new branches. For it is cramped, - it has not land as it once had.

The white man has come again, - shall we sell another piece of land - shall we let the tree under which our fathers sat, lose another and another root, and cause another and another branch to fall?

The orator enlarged upon the figure, and extended his illustration, frequently drawing a parallel between it and the nation, until every mind present was fully prepared to reject the overture for a treaty, and for the time being the nation, preserved its ancient inheritance. Well would it have been for the nation, if a similar result had awaited every subsequent attempt to purchase their birthright.

The labors of Mr. Kirkland among this people, were, in many instances, attended with the desired result; and a large portion of the nation, ultimately professed a speculative belief in the doctrines of christianity, and many of them bore witness by well ordered lives to the sincerity of their profession of that belief which is of the heart. Among the latter number, was the venerable Sconondoa, who for many years after the death of his spiritual father, waited with a christian composure, and even with a wish to depart, for the summons which should call him to meet him in the presence of their common Lord and Master. The strength of the attachment of this aged chief to his friend and guide to the pure faith of the gospel, may be inferred from his dying injunction, that his remains should be laid beside those of his christian father, that in the resurrection morn they might together waken to the sound of the archangel's trumpet, to meet their Saviour coming to judgment. The request was regarded, and the missionary and his disciple sleep together in the narrow house.

Shortly after the peace, the attention of individuals in Connecticut and Massachusetts was called to this vicinity, as a promising field for emigration. In the summer of the year 1784, Judge White, the first New England settler, with his sons, arrived at Whitestown, from Middletown, Conn., and erected a dwelling house. The next year he was joined by a number of settlers, and the name of Whitestown, very soon became known throughout New England, to designate the whole region lying near the central portion of the State. In the year 1786, the village of Clinton was settled by a colony of 20 families, and the tide of emigration increased from year to year, occupying neighborhoods in almost all parts of the present county of Oneida. I have already mentioned, that the state in remuneration to Mr. Kirkland for his services during the revolutionary was conferred upon him a valuable tract of land. This took place in the year 1788, and shortly after and about the year 1791, he conceived the project of establishing a seminary, which should prove a blessing alike to the people to whom he had given himself to be a teacher and a guide, and to the sons of his countrymen who were rapidly establishing themselves here, and converting the wilderness into the homes of civilization. The land granted to him by the State, furnished a suitable place as he believed, for the site of such an institution. This tract was bounded on one side upon the life of property, as it was then called, being the boundary between the Indian reservation and the land ceded to the white men. Situated thus at the threshold of the Indian territory, he looked upon it as just the point where the youth fresh from the schools of the white man, should meet the sons of the forest, and together unroll the book of knowledge.

At this distance of time, and with the knowledge of the changes which have taken place in the circumstances by the light of which he then viewed it, it is impossible for us to fail to admire the whole project as he prepared it for operation. Who could then believe, that a single generation would have hardly passed away, before the Oneidas, starting as it seemed from a savage state to that of a civilized and christian community, would have withered before the vices of civilization, ere its virtues had found a resting place among them, and that their story would have furnished so short and so mournful a page in the book of time, as has been written for them? And the philanthropist of that day might well hope that the foundation of such an institution would from age to age shed abroad healthful influences upon both races, and become a perpetual bond of brotherhood between the white and the red man.

With these views, Mr. Kirkland gave himself up to the project, expending his time and the means which Providence had placed in his hands, with unsparing zeal for its promotion. Through his exertions, a charter of incorporation was obtained for the institution, in 1793, under the name of the Hamilton Oneida Academy, and a fund raised in order to commence the erection of a suitable building for its operations. In 1794, the building which, after the elevation of the seminary to the rank of a college with the style of Hamilton College, for many years continued to be known as Oneida Hall, was raised and partially finished under the superintendence of our townsman Apollos Cooper. As soon as the requisite means could be obtained it was completed, and officers of instruction appointed, who at once established for it a character among the firsts in rank of the academies in the State. The fostering care of its founder never flagged in efforts to improve its condition and increase its usefulness, and prepare the way for its elevation to the rank of a college, which from its inception he had contemplated. And most deeply is this whole community indebted to him, for the blessings it has already dispensed upon the population of our land. And I may also remark, that whatever change the experience of the last twenty-five years may have dictated, as an improvement in the location of a college for the central portion of New York, under its present circumstances, and prospects for the future, yet during the life-time of its founder, there was no circumstance existing, which would have justified the preference of another location, or induced the belief, that the utility of the institution would be increased or promoted by its establishment upon a different site. His first object, to render it a seminary for the Indian as well as the white youth, required its establishment upon the frontier ground it occupied; and when yielding to the white man's offers, the sons of the forest retreated from the boundaries of their then territory, the local importance of no one of the existing villages in the vicinity was so much in advance of Clinton, as to warrant the belief, that it furnished a more desirable place for its operations. The death of Mr. Kirkland occurred in the spring of the year 1808. The place he occupied in the early history of Oneida County was most important, and one which will continue to exert an influence through all time. Jefferson desired that upon his tomb might be inscribed, "The founder of the University of Virginia." He could exult as he foresaw the day when the splendor of her halls and the magnificence of her appointments, would reflect lustre upon the name of even the author of the Declaration of Independence, and with a pardonable vanity, he desired to secure for it the glory. But the founder of Hamilton College, had a purer motive to actuate him in his enterprise. He asked no monument which should remind the careless of the Indian missionary, and keep his name fresh before the public gaze. He sought to establish a school to diffuse the blessings of learning, and the arts, and religion, upon the benighted son of the forest, as well as the youth from a more fortunate home; to open a well-spring of knowledge, where the humble as well as the lofty might quench their thirst for wisdom; and he little heeded what should be thought of the agent who effected the end. His name, no marble claimed to give to it its short-lived immortality, - no brass transmitted for another age to admire. And though in honor of its early friend, the town of his adoption now bears his name, many a year had his ashes slept in the cold bosom of the earth, before this simple yet affectionate tribute was paid to the memory of the apostle and benefactor of Oneida county.

Another name distinguished in the history of Oneida county, and occupying no obscure place in the catalogue of American patriots, is that of the late James Dean. The history of this individual and his agency in many of the events transpiring previous to and during the revolutionary war, would form a volume of deeply interesting and most thrilling incidents. A native of New England, and the child of religious parents, at the early age of eleven years, at the solicitation of a connection of his father's family, who as a clergyman had been engaged in the business of

Indian missions, his parents, like the mother of Samuel, devoted him to the service of the temple, as a herald of the Cross to the sons of the forest. In order to prepare their child for the peculiar duties he would be called upon to perform, by the advice of the relative I have mentioned, they concluded to send him even then in his early youth, to become acquainted with the Indian language and habits, and manners, and to grow up among and in contact with those among whom they intended his life should be spent. At this time, a branch of the Oneidas resided at a settlement called Onaquaga, situated on the Susquehanna, and to this place young Dean was sent to become a denizen of the forest. A missionary occasionally visited the post, and to him the early education of the subject of our notice, in the arts and letters of civilized life, was entrusted, while he was acquiring, with every day's growth, the accomplishments which go to make up the thoroughbred native of the wilderness. Here he continued until he arrived at a suitable age to enter Dartmouth College, with which institution very shortly after it received its charter he connected himself. He here completed his under graduate course in 1773, and was graduated in the third class which received its honors at that institution. Previous to his graduation, he accompanied a friend, the Rev. Sylvanus Ripley, afterwards the first professor of divinity of the college, on a mission to the Indians residing at Penobscot and on the Bay of Fundy. In a publication of the first president Whelock, printed at Hartford in 1773, he is spoken of in the following manner: -

"Mr. Dean has now finished his course of studies here, and upon finding, as I have already mentioned, that he may, with little expense, be able to preach to the Hurons freely in their own tongue, has determined, if God please, when he has perfected himself in the French tongue, to enter on a mission, and with a proper companion, preach as an itinerant, not only to the Six Nations, (with whom he lived many years from his youth,) but to the tribes that can understand him to a thousand miles, if such there are at that distance."

Such were the views and intentions with which he received his bachelor's diploma, and he accordingly commenced studies in theology, and continued them for several months, when he was regularly licensed as a preacher of the gospel, though, owing to the circumstances which afterwards have a change to his pursuits, he never was ordained to the sacred office.

It will be recollected, that the period at which I have now

arrived, was that of the commencement of the troubles which preceded the war of the Revolution. The odious duty upon tea was exciting in America the deepest feeling of opposition to the administration of affairs in the mother country, and resolutions of resistance to its execution, amounting to open rebellion, were publicly passed in the popular assemblies held in every colony. The opposition to the entrance of ships bearing cargoes of tea into New York, Philadelphia and most of the ports of the colonies, the destruction of the tea in Boston harbor in the winter of '73-'74, and the measures of the government thereupon in the passage of the bill shutting up the port of Boston, as a punishment for the insult to the royal authority; the act of parliament altering the whole form of government in Massachusetts, and authorizing the removal of persons accused of murder or of any capital offence in aiding the enforcement of these laws by the magistracy, to the mother country for trial, early in the year 1774 had increased the feeling of excitement which pervaded all the colonies, and rendered universal the belief that a crisis was approaching, in which it would become necessary for all the colonies to defend their rights with strong arm. At this period, when the first continental Congress was assembling at Philadelphia, and the leading citizens of each colony were endeavoring to ascertain the sentiments of all classes of people relative to the contest that was portending, the peculiar talents and qualifications which his education had afforded him, recommended the subject of our notice to the continental authorities, as a suitable person to ascertain the feeling of the Indians in New York and Canada, and the part they would probably take in the event of a war with the mother country. In order to disguise the object of his mission, it was arranged that he should assume the business of an Indian trader, and he was accordingly furnished with such goods as were then carried into the Indian country by that class of persons, and with letters, bills of parcels and other documents from a well-known house at Boston at that time engaged in the traffic, in order to authenticate his assumed character. Thus prepared, he set out upon an expedition to visit the Six Nations, and the various branches of the different tribes composing them, or connected with them living in Canada. In the course of his travels in Lower Canada, he was arrested by the British authorities as a spy, and carried to Quebec; but by a prudent and careful bearing of himself, aided by the papers which he carried, he was discharged and returned home, having successfully accomplished the object of his mission.

As the troubles increased in the colonies, his services became of great importance to the country, in order to conciliate the Indian tribes, and as a means of communication with them. An adopted son of the Oneidas, educated in all their habits and customs, and skilled, moreover, in all the white man's knowledge, the nation regarded him with more than parental affection, and to the regard which they entertained for him and their religious teacher, Mr. Kirkland, may be wholly attributed their friendship for the colonists, while most of the other portions of the Six Nations adhered to the arms of the mother country. On the final outbreak of hostilities in 1775, and the assignment of the command of the northwestern frontier of New York to General Schuyler, Mr. Dean was appointed to the office of Indian Agent, with the staff rank of major in the army, and during the whole war of the revolution he continued his services to the country in that capacity. For most of the time, his duties were performed in the neighborhood of the Oneidas. A very considerable portion of the war he was stationed at Fort Stanwix, the site of the present village of Rome, and by virtue of his office, superintended the intercourse with the Indians, and obtaining of all information through them. By means of an Indian scout in his employment, known to the early settlers of the county, and indeed remembered by the writer as Saucy Nick, he obtained information of the very hour that the attack was to be made upon Cherry Valley, previous to the massacre at that ill-fated settlement, and in sufficient time to have Colonel Alden, the commander of the post, apprised of it. The intelligence was transmitted to him through the commandant of the garrison at Fort Stanwix, but the ill-fated Alden, disregarding the news and sneering at it as an Indian humbug, permitted the inhabitants of the settlement peacefully and unalarmed and unprotected to retire to rest on the night of the attack, and before morning, paid with his own life, and the lives of those he was placed to protect, the price of his rash incredulity.

The siege of Fort Stanwix, and the battle of Oriskany, occurred during an absence of Mr. Dean down the Mohawk. On his return with the brigade commanded by General Arnold intended for the relief of the garrison, he passed the battle ground, still strewn with the corpses of those who had fallen in the conflict, blackening unburied where they fell. The brigade paused and performed the last sad office to their compatriots, and when the earth had received their remains, proceeded to its destination. The subject of our notice subsequently was attached to the expedition of Gen.

Sullivan in the western part of New York, and was present at the battle at Newtown - now Elmira. A manuscript journal and narrative of this expedition, prepared by him with great care, was for many years preserved by his family, but has unfortunately been destroyed. The information it contained would have been extremely valuable, and serve to throw much light upon the manners and condition of the Six Nations at that period. At the close of the war, the Oneidas granted him a tract of land two miles square, lying on the Wood Creek west of Rome, to which he removed in 1784 and commenced its improvement. He here continued two years, when he effected an exchange with the nation for the tract of land lying in Westmoreland, known as Dean's Patent, and removed to his late residence upon it in 1786, where he continued to reside until his death. Upon the cession to the State in 1788, of the lands lying outside of the line of property as it is called, the State, in view of his meritorious services during the war, confirmed the grant to him by patent, under which a portion of the land is held by his family at the present day.

Two or three years after the removal of Mr. Dean from Wood Creek to the latter place, an incident occurred which furnishes a parallel to the rescue of Captain Smith by Pocahontas in the early days of Virginia. An institution existed among the Indians for the punishment of a murderer, answering in some respects to the Jewish code. It became the duty of the nearest relative of the deceased to pursue him, and avenge his brother's death. In case the murder was perpetrated by a member of a different tribe, the offence demanded that the tribe of the murdered man should require the blood of some member of the offending tribe. This was regarded as a necessary atonement, and as absolutely requisite to the happiness of the deceased in the world of spirits, and a religious duty, and not as a mere matter of vengeful gratification. At the period to which I have referred, an Indian had been murdered by some unknown white man, who had escaped. The chiefs thereupon held a consultation at Oneida to determine what was to be done. Their deliberations were held in secret, but through the friendship of one of the number, Mr. Dean was advised of what was going on. From the office that he had held, and the high standing he maintained among the white men, it was urged in the council that he was the proper person to sacrifice in atonement of the offence committed. The question was, however, a very difficult one to dispose of. He had been adopted into the tribe, and was held to be a son, and it was argued by many of the chiefs that he could now be no more responsible for the offence than one of the natives of the tribe, and that his sacrifice would not furnish the proper atonement. For several days the matter was debated and no decision was arrived at. While it was undetermined, he continued to hope for the best, and his friendly informant kept him constantly advised of all that was done. At first he reflected upon the propriety of his leaving the country and escaping from the danger. But his circumstances, together with the hope of a favorable issue of the question in the council, induced him to remain. He had erected a small house which he was occupying with his wife and two children, one an infant, and it was idle to think of removing them without exciting observation and perhaps causing a sacrifice of all. As the council continued its session for several days, his hopes of a favorable decision brightened. He however kept the whole matter to himself, not even mentioning it to his wife, and prepared himself for any emergency which might befall him. One night after he had retired to bed, he was awoke by the sound of the death whoop, at a short distance from his house. He then for the first time communicated to his wife his fears that a party were approaching to take his life. He enjoined it upon her to remain quiet with her children in the room where they slept, while he would receive the council in an adjoining one and endeavor to avert their determination, trusting to Providence for the result. He met the Indians at the door, and seated them in the outer room. There were eighteen, and all chiefs or head men of the nation. The senior chief informed him that they had come to sacrifice him for the murder of their brother, and that he must now prepare to die. He replied to them at length, claiming that he was an adopted son of the Oneidas; that it was unjust to require his blood for the wrong committed by a wicked white man; that he was not ready to die, and that he could not leave his wife and children unprovided for. The council listened to him with profound gravity and attention, and when he sat down, one of the chiefs replied to him. He rejoined, and used every argument his ingenuity could devise in order to reverse their sentence. The debate continued a long time, and the hope of escape grew fainter and fainter as it proceeded. At length he had nearly abandoned himself to the doom they had resolved upon, when he heard the pattering of a footstep without the door. All eyes were fixed upon the door. It opened and a squaw entered. She was the wife of the senior chief, and at the time of Mr. Dean's adoption into the tribe in his boyhood, she had taken him as her son. The entrance of a woman into a solemn council, was, by Indian etiquette, at war with all propriety. She, however, took her place near the door, and all looked on in silence. A moment after, another footstep was heard, and another Indian woman entered the council. This was a sister of the former, and she too was the wife of a chief then present. Another pause ensued, and a third entered. Each of the three stood wrapped closely in her blanket, but said nothing. At length the presiding chief addressed them, telling them to begone and leave the chiefs to go on with their business. The wife replied, that the council must change their determination and let the good white man - their friend - her own adopted son, alone. The command to be gone was repeated, when each of the Indian women threw off her blanket and showed a knife in her extended hand, and declared that if one hair of the white man's head was touched, they would each bury their knives in their own heart's blood. The strangeness of the whole scene overwhelmed with amazement each member of the council, and regarding the unheard of resolution of the women to interfere in the matter as a sort of manifestation of the will of the Great Spirit that the white man's life should not be taken, their previous decree was reversed on the spot, and the life of their victim preserved.

Shortly after the erection of the county of Herkimer in 1791, Mr. Dean was appointed a judge of the county courts, in which office he was continued until the erection of the county of Oneida, when he was appointed to a similar station in this county, and retained the office by successive appointments, and occasionally served as a member of the state legislature, until the year 1813, when he retired from public life, and devoted his remaining days to the enjoyment of domestic quiet, and a preparation for the time of his departure. This event took place in September, 1832.

The lives of few men present more claims to the affection, respect and veneration of their countrymen than that of Judge Dean. From the circumstances of his youth and education, calculated to exercise a most useful and important part in his country's service, he was early called to act in emergencies requiring the display of great wisdom, strong fortitude and sincere and devoted patriotism, in all of which he showed himself equal to the demand. As a citizen, his amiable deportment, his benevolence and his unwavering integrity, endeared him to all who knew him. As a magistrate and legislator, his strong and well-balanced mind, well stored with sound learning and the wisdom which is begotten of experience and extensive observation, commanded universal respect within the sphere in which he moved.

In connection with the sketches I have given of the characters of the Rev. Mr. Kirkland and Judge Dean, I propose to notice the siege of Fort Stanwix and the battle of Oriskany, - events which have made the soil of Oneida classic ground, and which hold an important place in the history of the American Revolution. I will detain you for a few moments upon the subject, and then close my remarks for this evening.

Fort Stanwix was originally erected in the year 1758, during the French war, as it is commonly called. It occupied a position commanding the carrying place between the navigable waters of the Mohawk and Wood Creek, and was regarded as the key to the communication between Canada and the settlements on the Mohawk. It was originally a square Fort, having four bastions surrounded by a broad and deep ditch, with a covert way and glacis. In the centre of the ditch a row of perpendicular pickets was planted and another horizontal row fixed around the ramparts. After the French war, the fortification had been permitted to go into decay; and at the commencement of hostilities with the mother country, it needed thorough repairs in order to make it useful for the purposes intended. Upon Gen. Schuyler being ordered to the command of the northwestern frontier, he placed Col. Gansevoort in command of the fort with a small garrison, and commenced the work of placing the fortification in a situation for resistance. Early in the summer of the year 1777, the enemy's plan of the northern campaign against the revolutionary forces became understood, and the necessity of preventing its successful issue most deeply felt. The plan contemplated the complete subjugation of New York, by a combination of movements in three different directions, in the hope that by severing New England from the other States, a more easy victory would be afforded to the royal arms. In order to do this, General Burgoyne was to descend from Montreal by way of Lake Champlain, and force his way to Albany. In the meantime, a detachment of the invading forces under the command of Colonel St. Leger, consisting of 200 British troops and a regiment of loyalists under Sir John Johnson, together with a large body of Indians in the employment of the royal government, were to pass up the St. Lawrence to Lake Ontario, and by the way of Oswego, Oneida Lake and Wood Creek, obtain possession of Fort Stanwix, and passing down the Mohawk, form a junction with the main army at Albany. The combined force was then to proceed onward to meet Sir Henry Clinton, who was to press up the Hudson River, with the forces under his command, and occupy all the fortresses upon its banks. As early as the 3rd of July, (1777) it became apparent to the garrison at Fort Stanwix that hostile Indians were prowling about the fort. Precautions were taken to render the fortifications as secure as possible, and on the first day of August everyt.ling was in a fit state of preparation for the enemy. There were, nevertheless, as yet, two things most essential in the defense of a fortification to be supplied - ammunition and provisions. An express, however, arrived in the camp on that day, bringing notice that a supply of these articles was approaching in batteaus accompanied by a guard of 200 men. The supplies arrived on the second of August in the afternoon, and while the last boat was unlading the enemy made his appearance near the landing place. The garrison now consisted of seven hundred and fifty men; and an examination of their stores showed that their provisions and ammunition would permit them to hold out six weeks, by husbanding well their resources, and firing but nine cannon per day. A demand of surrender was now made by the British commanding officer, and indignantly refused by the garrison. The siege then commenced with great activity on the part of the enemy. Upon hearing of the investment of the fort, General Herkimer, (Hercheimer] who then commanded the militia of Tryon county (as the whole territory afterwards known as Montgomery county, and including all the State west of Schenectady county, was then called), collected a force of about eight hundred militia from the Dutch and German settlements below this, and started with them to the relief of the besieged. On the evening of the 5th of August, General Herkimer arrived at the Oriskany creek, and sent two expresses with letters to Colonel Gansevoort, informing him of his approach and where he then was, and desiring cannon to be fired to inform him of the safe arrival of his expresses. He also requested that a sally might be made immediately on their arrival, to effect a diversion of the enemy's forces, in order to favor his approach to the fort. The expresses arrived safely in camp on the forenoon of the 6th, about eleven o'clock. The cannon were immediately fired as a signal to Gen. Herkimer, and a force of two hundred and fifty men with a piece of artillery detailed under Colonel Willett, the second in command, to make a sally. A thunder shower, of which I shall again have occasion to speak, coming up, detained it for an hour. The sally from the fort was

Rome Historical Society

Gen. Nicholas Herkimer (1728-1777)

most fortunate. The camps of Sir John Johnson and of the Indians were taken, their owners put to flight, and the whole camp equippage, clothing, blankets and stores, the officer's baggage, memoranda and papers, together with five British flags secured and carried into the fort, and all without the loss of a single man. The British flag were immediately displayed beneath the American ensign as trophies of the victory.

Not so fortunate, however, was the fate of the gallant band marching to the relief of their countrymen. Colonel St. Leger learning of their approach, detached a portion of the force under his command with a party of Indians to lie in ambush and intercept them. The path then leading from Oriskany to the fort passed the gulph which constitutes the present boundary of Rome, at the distance of twenty or thirty rods north of the present road to Rome at that point. The ambuscade commenced in this gulph, and the enemy were lying concealed on both sides of the path for some distance above it. On the morning of the sixth, General Herkimer, after waiting until about 8 o'clock, and hearing no discharge of cannon from the fort, supposed his express might not have succeeded in reaching it, and proceeded with his command. The column consisting wholly of militia men, and not expecting an immediate attack, entered the ambuscade in open order and unprepared for action, and nearly half of the whole body had passed the gulph, when the Indian war whoop became the signal of attack, and one of the most bloody conflicts of modern times ensued. The attack was general and from every quarter. Thrown into confusion at the onset, and without the habits of military discipline, necessary to enable them to rally in the fury of the strife, a portion of the militia who had not reached the ambuscade fled, while with the remainder the action became a melee of single contests, the militia forming a circle around their leader, and maintaining their ground, and gallantly resisting the attack, until the violent shower of which I have spoken commenced, when the enemy withdrew to his camp. In the contest, one hundred and sixty militia men fell dead on the field, and a very large number were wounded and removed by the survivors to Herkimer. Among the number of the wounded was General Herkimer. He received a bullet about six inches below his knee, which splintered the bone. His leg was afterwards amputated, and it is supposed that he might have recovered, but in the inflammation ensuing upon the amputation, he became delirious, and tore the bandages from the leg and in consequence bled to death.

After the unsuccessful issue of the attempt to relieve the besieged, Colonel St. Leger again sent a flag of truce with a demand to the garrison to surrender, promising protection in case the summons should be complied with, and threatening the fury of his savage allies in case it was refused. The demand was spurned at and the investing army defied. It was then deemed advisable to attempt a communication with the settlements and the procuring of a reinforcement, and Colonel Willet and Lieutenant Stockwell of the garrison, volunteered to go on the hazardous expedition. They left the fort on the evening of the 10th of August, and succeeded by a most fatiguing and perilous march through the country lying seven or eight miles northward of the Mohawk, in reaching the German settlements of Herkimer. They there learned that Gen. Learned had received orders to repair, with a brigade of Massachusetts troops from the vicinity of the Cahoes, to meet Gen. [Benedict] Arnold with another force, and together proceed, under the command of Arnold, to the relief of the garrison. On hearing of the approach of Arnold with his force, the Indians co-operating with Col. St. Leger became dissatisfied, and threatened to leave. At this juncture, a tory (Tost Schuyler) who had been taken prisoner, and who could speak the Indian language, was released upon condition that he should go among the Indians and represent the force of the relieving army. To secure his fidelity his brother was detained as a hostage, with a threat that he should be hung in case Tost was treacherous. The intelligence of Schuyler produced in them general distrust and alarm, and Gen. St. Leger, on the 22nd of August, after having vigilantly and energetically prosecuted the siege for twenty days, was forced to raise it and retreat to Oswego. The result so creditable to the garrison and the officers conducting it, was also productive of most important consequences, whether we regard it as saving the settlements on the Mohawk from the savages of a ruthless and indictive enemy, or in its effect upon the public sentiment here and in the mother country. "Nothing," says the British Annual Register for 1777, "could have been more untoward in the present situation of affairs than the unfortunate issue of this expedition. The Americans represented this and the affair at Bennington as great and glorious victories. Nothing could exceed their exultation and confidence. Gansevoort and Willet, with Starke and Warner, (heroes of Bennington) were ranked among those who were considered the saviours of their country."

LECTURE II

In continuing the subject with which I occupied your attention in my former lecture, I will next introduce to your notice an individual, who, although not an inhabitant of Oneida county, deserves from its chronicler more than a passing notice. I speak of Heinrich Staring, for many years First Judge of Herkimer county while it comprehended within its limits the present county of Oneida, and the first individual who held that office. In his case have the words of the great master of dramatic poetry been signally verified:

> "The evil that men do, lives after them;
> "The good, is oft interred with their bones."

Although for many years occupying most important public stations, and exercising an influence most salutary during an eventful period of our national history, little is known of him by the present generation, save the anecdotes which the lovers of fun of his day chose to invent and circulate in ridicule of his peculiarities. Heinrich Staring was a native of the Mohawk Valley, and was born about eleven miles below this city, very early after the settlement of the German Flatts. Little is now known of his early history. At the commencement of the Revolutionary War, we find him a militia officer, and regarded by the royal party as a most important and influential personage in his neighborhood. He was present at the battle of Oriskany, and from that period held the office of colonel of the Tryon county militia during the remainder of the war. Possessing great shrewdness, strong common sense, and unflinching intrepidity, he enjoyed the unlimited confidence of the German and Dutch settlers on the Mohawk, and became a prominent object for seizure by the enemy. A great number of anecdotes illustrative of the extraordinary means that were used by the enemy he had to deal with to procure his person or destroy him, might be related. My plan for this evening, however, will permit me to give you but a single one. The story was told to my informant from the lips of the old man several years after the war. The event took place sometime late in November, and about the year 1778 or 1779. He had, for some purpose, gone into the woods at some distance from his home, and while there, by chance, came suddenly upon a party of hostile Indians, who, during those years, were frequently prowling about the settlements on the Mohawk, and occasionally making murderous incursions among the inhabitants. Before he became fully aware of their presence he had got so completely in their power that flight or resistance were out of the question. He was seized with every demonstration of hellish delight, and rapidly hurried away in a contrary direction from his home and southward of the Mohawk, until his captors supposed themselves out of the reach of pursuit, when they directed their march westward, and at night reached a small uninhabited wigwam at a little more than a quarter of a mile from the right bank of the Oriskany Creek above Clinton, in what is now called Brothertown. This wigwam consisted of two rooms, separated from each other by a partition of logs. Into the larger of these there opened an outside door which furnished the only entrance to the house. Another door communicated from the larger to the smaller room. The latter had one window, a small square hole of less than a foot high by about two feet wide, placed nearly six feet above the floor. The whole structure was of logs, substantially built. The Indians examined the smaller room, and concluded that by securely fastening their prisoner hand and foot, they could safely keep him there until morning. They therefore bound his hands behind him with withes, and then fastened his ankles together in the same manner, and laid him thus bound in the small room, while they built a fire in the larger one, and commenced a consultation concerning the disposition of him. Staring, though unable to speak the Indian language, was sufficiently acquainted with it to understand their deliberations, and he lay listening intently to their conversation. The whole party were unanimous in the decision that he must be put to death, but the manner of doing this in the way best calculated to make the white warrior cry like a cowardly squaw, was a question of high importance, and one which it required a good deal of deliberation to settle satisfactorily to all his captors. At length, however, it was agreed that he should be burned alive on the following morning, and preparations were accordingly made for the diabolical sports of a savage auto dafe. During the deliberation, the horrible fate that awaited him suggested to Colonel Staring the question of the possibility of an escape. As he lay on the ground in the wigwam, he could see the window I have spoken of, and he determined to make an effort to release himself from the withes which bound him, and endeavor to effect a passage through it without alarming his savage keeper. Before they had sunk to rest, he had so far succeeded as to release one of his hands from its fastenings sufficiently to enable him to slip his wrist from it. On finding that he could do this, he feigned sleep; and when the Indians came in to examine and see if all was safe, they retired exulting with a fiend-like sneer, that their victim was sleeping his last sleep. They then all laid down on the ground in the larger room, to go to sleep. Staring waited until all had for a long time become quiet, when, slipping his hand from the withes, he was enabled silently to release his ankles, and by climbing up the side of the house by the aid of the logs, to escape from the window without creating an alarm. In the attempt, and while releasing his ankles from the withes, he had necessarily taken off his shoes, and had forgotten to secure them with him. He was now outside of the wigwam, barefoot, at a distance of five and twenty miles from his home, without a guide or a path, hungry, and in a frosty night in November, and with a band of enemies seeking his heart's blood lying ready to spring upon him. But he was once more free from their clench, and this one thought was nerve, and strength and food - was all he needed to call into action his every power. He stole with cautious silence from the wigwam, directing his course toward the creek, and increasing his gait as he left his captors and got beyond the danger of alarming them. He had got about half way to the creek, and had begun to flatter himself that his whole escape was accomplished, when he heard a shout from the wigwam, and immediately the bark of the Indian dogs in pursuit. He then plunged on at the top of his speed, and knowing that while on the land, the dogs would follow on his track, in order to baffle their pursuit, as soon as he reached the creek, he jumped in, and ran down stream in the channel. For some time he heard the shouts of his late masters, and the baying of their hounds in the pursuit; and now that he had reached the water where their dogs could not track him, he laughed out - right as he ran, in thinking of the disappointment they would feel when they arrived at the bank. The fear of the faggot and all its accompanying tortures, furnished a stimulus to every muscle, and he urged on his flight until he heard no more of his enemies, and became satisfied that they had given up their pursuit. He deemed it prudent, however, to continue his course in the bed of the creek, until he should reach a path which led from Oneida to old Fort Schuyler - a mud fort, built on the present site of this city during the French war, and which was situated between Main street and the banks of the river, a little eastward of Second street. The path crossed the Oriskany about half a mile westward of where the village of Clinton now stands. He then took this path and pursued

Rome Historical Society

Fort Schuyler

his course. I have mentioned that in his haste to escape, he forgot his shoes. He had on a pair of wool stockings, but in running on the gravel in the creek, they soon became worn out, and the sharp pebbles cut his feet. In this difficulty he bethought him of a substitute for shoes, in the coat he wore, which, fortunately, was made of a thick heavy serge. He cut off the sleeves of this at his elbows, and drew them upon his feet, and thus protected them from injury. But he used to say he soon found this was robbing Peter to pay Paul, for in the severity of the night, his arms became chilled and almost frozen. He reached the landing at this place just in the gray dawn of the morning, and cautiously reconnoitering in order to ascertain whether anyone was in the fort, which was frequently used as a campground, he satisfied himself that no one was in the neighborhood. In doing this he fortunately discovered a canoe which had floated down the stream and lodged in the willows which grew on the edge of the bank. He instantly took possession of it, and by a vigorous use of the paddles, with the aid of the current, succeeded in reaching his home with his little bark in the middle of the forenoon.

In my former lecture, I mentioned the fact that the whole of the State westward of a line drawn through the western boundary of Schenectady county, previous to and during the revolutionary war, constituted the county of Tryon, being named in honor of Governor Tryon, the last colonial Governor of New York. The name of a royalist, however, sounding harsh to American ears, immediately after the war, the legislature, by an act passed in April, 1784, changed its name to Montgomery, in honor of the memory of Gen. Richard Montgomery, who fell in the attack on Quebec. The county continued to retain all its territory until 1789, when the emigration from the older parts of the country had so increased the population in the eastern portion of the State, that the county of Ontario was erected, comprehending all the territory lying west of a line drawn from the southeast corner of the present county of Seneca northward to the Lake Ontario.

On the 16th of February, 1791, the county of Montgomery was still further divided, and the counties of Tioga, Otsego and Herkimer formed; the county of Herkimer, comprising all the territory lying between the present counties of Montgomery and Otsego on the east, and the Cayuga Lake on the west, and bounded northerly and southerly by the north and south boundaries of the State. By the act erecting the county it was provided, that a court of common pleas and general sessions should be held in the county twice each year, and at the Church in Herkimer, until other legislative provisions should be made concerning the matter. Another provision of this act seems, to the observer of the present day, very remarkable, and shows as strikingly as any other fact, the rapidity with which our country has sprung from its first beginnings to its present condition. It was enacted, that it should not be the duty of the Justices of the Supreme Court to hold a Circuit Court once in each year in either of the three new counties then formed, unless in their judgment, they should deem it proper and necessary. No court in a territory now constituting the greater portion of four judicial circuits, and furnishing sufficient business for sixty circuit courts in each year, besides nearly one hundred and twenty terms of courts of common pleas, and sixteen of the court of chancery!

In organizing the court of common pleas for Herkimer county, Colonel Staring was appointed its first Judge. It is not supposed nor pretended, that any peculiar qualifications or fitness for the office, recommended him for the appointment. His honest and strong, but uncultivated mind, had never been schooled to threading the mazes of legal science; and indeed, he had enjoyed few of even the most common advantages of education. But he possessed the confidence of his fellow citizens for his sterling integrity, strong common sense, and tried and approved patriotism; and these qualifications were regarded by the venerable George Clinton, then Governor of the State, as sufficient to warrant his appointment to the office; and in forming our opinion of the appointment, we should take into consideration the fact, that at that period in the history of this State, there was scarcely to be found a court of common pleas which could boast a lawyer in its catalogue of judges. The judges of these tribunals were almost without exception, taken from the respectable farmers and mechanics of the land, and were men who made no pretensions to a knowledge of the artificial rules which go to make up what we professional gentlemen are want to call the perfection of reason; but who decided the questions coming before them by the plain principles of common sense, and their own views of right and wrong. And it is no disparagement to the fair fame of the courts of common pleas of that day to assert, that in which Judge Staring presided, was in no respect inferior to its sister tribunals. And I have the authority of a lawyer once holding a distinguished rank at the bar of this State, and whose partialities, all who remember him will bear me witness, betrayed, at least, no especial leaning to the Dutch, I mean the late Erastus Clark, in the opinion, that for strength of mind, correctness of judgment, and unflinching integrity, he never knew a man who, with so limited an education, in the station which he held, could have been regarded his superior. A great many anecdotes illustrative of his simplicity of character are related. I will merely revert to one well known to many of my hearers. Under the insolvent laws of the day, a debtor could make an application to a judge of the county courts for a discharge from his debts, upon making an assignment of all his property. One day an unfortunate debtor applied to him to obtain the relief afforded by the statute, and having prepared and duly executed his assignment, waited the signature of the judge to perfect his discharge. Well, said he, have you got all things ready. Yes, replied the debtor; every thing is prepared - all you have to do is sign my discharge. Very well, said the judge, have you paid all your debts? O no, said the debtor; if I had I should not apply for the benefit of the statute. But, replied the judge, I can't sign the paper till you have paid all your debts: you must pay your debts first. Upon this point he was inexorable, and the applicant was forced to seek elsewhere the relief he desired.

On the 19th of January, 1793, an act was passed authorizing every alternate term of the court of common pleas of Herkimer county to be held at such place in Whitestown, as should by the courts be directed by orders to be entered in the minutes. The first court held in this county under this provision was held in a barn, in New Hartford, belonging to the late Judge Sanger, (New Hartford then forming a part of the town of Whitestown), in the month of October, in the year 1793, Judge Staring presiding, and the late Judge Platt, then clerk of the county of Oneida, officiating as clerk. The sheriff of Herkimer county at that day was a Colonel Colbraith - an Irishman, who, in the war, had done some service to his adopted country, and had acquired his title as a militia officer since the peace. His education had not been conducted with especial reference to the usages of what is technically called good society; and indeed, his manners bore unequivocal evidence that they originated from a native mine of genuine good humor and a most capacious soul, rather than from the arbitrary rules of a professor of polite breeding. A gentleman who attended the court as a spectator, informed me, that the day was one of the damp, chilly days we frequently have in October, and that in the afternoon and when it was nearly night, in order to comfort themselves in their by no means very well appointed court room, and to keep their vital blood at a temperature at which it would continue to circulate, some of the gentleman of the bar had induced the sheriff to procure from a neighboring inn, a jug of spirits. This, it must be remembered, was before the invention of temperance societies, and we may not, therefore, pass too hasty an opinion upon the propriety of the measure. Upon the jug appearing in court, it was passed around the bar table, and each of the learned counsellors in his turn upraised the elegant vessel and decanted into his mouth, by the simplest process imaginable, so much as he deemed a sufficient dose of the delicious fluid. While the operation was going on, the dignitaries on the bench, who were no doubt, suffering quite as much from the chilliness of the weather as their brethern of the bar, had a little consultation, when the first Judge announced to the audience that the court saw no reason why they should continue to hold open there any longer and freeze to death, and desired the crier forthwith to adjourn the court. Before, however, this funtionary could commence with a single "Hear ye," Colonel Colbraith jumped up, catching as he rose, the jug from the lawyer who was complimenting its contents, and holding it up towards the bench, hastily ejaculated - "Oh no, no, no, Judge - don't adjourn yet - take a little gin, Judge - that will keep you warm - 'tani time to adjourn yet"; and suiting the action to the word, he handed His Honor the jug. It appeared that there was force in the Sheriff's advice; for the order to adjourn was revoked, and the business went on.

Judge Staring continued in office until after the erection of Oneida county, and finally resigned his office shortly after that event. His death took place after the year 1800, but at what precise period I have been unable to learn.

In my former lecture, I incidentally mentioned the settlement of Whitestown in the year 1784. I should, however, remark that some years previous two men, named Roof and Brodock, from the German Flatts, had established themselves with their families at the landing place on the Mohawk, in the vicinity of Fort Stanwix, and gained a livelihood by assisting in the transportation of the goods destined for the Indian trade, across the carrying place from the river to Wood Creek. They held no title to their lands, but occupied them under a contract for their purchase from Oliver Delancy, one of the proprietors of the Oriskany patent, who was afterwards attainted of treason as an adherent to the enemy. This little out post was, however, broken up during the war, but after the return of peace, the settlers returned and took up their residence in their former home. This was, in fact, the first white settlement in central New York; but the great work of colonizing this region, and converting the wilderness into a garden, can hardly be said to have been commenced by these early emigrants. The pioneer in this enterprise, and he who led the way for the sons of the pilgrims into the as yet unbroken forest, was the late Hugh White. In this individual were combined many striking traits of character, eminently calculated to fit him for the post he occupied. Possessing an uncommon vigor of intellect, an ardent spirit of enterprise, an intrepidity and energy that is rarely to be met with, and a perseverance and devotion to his purpose that regarded no obstacle as insurmountable, few men could have compared with him, in the proper endowments of the frontier settler. His native place was Middletown, Connecticut, where he had all his life resided up to the period of his emigration. He had then attained the age of 51 years. Immediately after the war, he had by purchase, become one of the proprietors of Sadaquada Patent, and held it jointly with Zephaniah Platt, the father of the late Judge Platt, Ezra L'Hommedieu and Melancthon Smith. By an arrangement between the proprietors, it was agreed that they should meet at the land in the summer of 1784, and make a survey and partition of it. He determined at once to make it his home, and accordingly, in the month of May of that year, he left his native place, accompanied by his four sons, all of whom had arrived at manhood, a daughter and daughter-in-law. The party made passage by water to Albany, there crossed the carrying place to Schenectady, and procuring a batteau, ascended the Mohawk. In the month of June they arrived at the mouth of the Sauquoit Creek. They there erected a shanty for their temporary accommodation, while surveying and dividing the lands. This being done, the owners drew for their several shares, and the lot which fell to Judge White being all interval land, he purchased of Smith the lot drawn by him in its rear, which extended to the south line of the patent upon the hill. The whole constituted fifteen hundred acres, comprehending all the land lying on both sides of the Sauquoit Creek, from the corner formed by the road leading to the Oneida factory, to that at Berry's in Whitesboro, and extending from the bank of the Mohawk back to the hills more than a mile southward from the latter village. Upon obtaining the partition, he at once proceeded to the erection of a log house. A site was soon fixed upon on the bank which forms the eastern boundary of the village green in

Whitesboro, and about six rods from the left side of the road as you rise the bank on entering the village. This was just on the right hand of the Indian path which led from old Fort Schuyler, the site of our city, to Fort Stanwix, and which path soon became, and for several years continued to be, the only road between the two points. The house was erected, and he remained there with his sons until the winter, cutting away the forest, and making preparations for the operations of the ensuing season. In the January succeeding, he returned to Connecticut and brought his wife and the remainder of his family. At this time, we can with difficulty estimate the trials, and perplexities, and privations which the new settler had then to encounter. The various inventions contrived within the last half century to relieve the inconveniencies, and provide for the comfort of those who go forth into the wilderness, have rendered emigration to a new and uncultivated and uninhabited country, a matter of comparatively little hardship; and we now bid farewell to the friend bound with his family to the distant fields of the far west, and expecting to plant his standard scores of miles beyond the smoke of any neighbor's cottage, and many hundreds, and even thousands, from the home of his childhood and the faces which are familiar to him, very much as we exchange salutations with our neighbor, who is leaving his home on a visit for a week.

At this period, the Indian title had not been extinguished to any portion of the country westward of the line of property, running from a point near the northwest corner of the town of Bridgewater northwesterly to a point on Wood Creek four or five miles west of Rome, and forming the western boundary of Coxe's Patent, as laid down on the maps of the county. Most of the Oneidas, it was known, had, during the war which was just terminated, maintained their professions of friendship for the Americans in a consistent and honorable manner. But the fact was well understood, that their confederate tribes in the Six Nations still felt the smart of the blow inflicted upon them five years before, in the expedition made into their country by the army under General Sullivan, and secretly desired an opportunity to take vengeance upon the countrymen of those who then chastised them. This rendered his position that of a frontier settler, and required of him the exercise of much prudence and sagacity in his intercourse with his neighbors. He soon acquired their good will, and had the good fortune to inspire them with very exalted ideas of his character and prowess. For many years after his arrival at

Whitestown, quite a number of the Oneidas resided at Oriskany, and an Indian clearing of over two hundred acres, now forming a part of the farms known as the "Green Farms," had been formed there long anterior to the Revolutionary War. His intercourse with this little settlement was marked by an incident which illustrates the feeling that was entertained for him by its inhabitants. An old chief, named Han Yerry, who, during the war, had acted with the royal party, and now resided at Oriskany in a log wigwam which stood on this side of the creek, just back of the house, until recently, occupied by Mr. Charles Green, one day called at Judge White's with his wife, and a mulatto woman who belonged to him, and who acted as his interpreter. After conversing with him a little while, the Indian asked him - Are you my friend? Yes, said he. Well, then, said the Indian, do you believe I am your friend? Yes, Han Yerry, replied he; I believe you are. The Indian then rejoined - Well, if you are my friend, and you believe I am your friend, I will tell you what I want, and then I shall know whether you speak true words. And what is it that you want? said Mr. White. The Indian then pointed to a little grandchild, the daughter of one of his sons, then between two and three years old, and said, - my squaw wants to take this papoose home with us to stay one night, and bring her home tomorrow: if you are my friend, you will now show me. The feelings of the grandfather at once uprose in his bosom, and the child's mother started with horror and alarm at the thought of entrusting her darling prattler with the rude tenants of the forest. The question was full of interest. On the one hand, the necessity of placing unlimited confidence in the savage, and entrusting the welfare and the life of his grandchild with him; on the other, the certain enmity of a man of influence and consequence in his nation, and one who had been the open enemy of his countrymen in their recent struggle. But he made the decision with a sagacity that showed that he properly estimated the character of the person he was dealing with. He believed that by placing implicit confidence in him, he should command the sense of honor which seems peculiar to the uncontaminated Indian. He told him to take the child; and as the mother, scarcely suffering it to be parted from her, relinquished it into the hands of the old man's wife, he soothed her fears with his assurances of confidence in their promises. That night, however, was a long one; and during the whole of the next morning many and often were the anxious glances cast up the pathway leading from Oriskany, if possible, to discover the Indians and their little charge, upon their return to its home. But no Indians came in sight. It at length became high noon: all a mother's fears were aroused: she could scarcely be restrained from rushing in pursuit of her loved one. But her father represented to her the gross indignity which a suspicion of their intentions would arouse in the breast of the chief; and half frantic though she was, she was restrained. The afternoon slowly wore away, and still nothing was seen of her child. The sun had nearly reached the horizon, and the mother's heart had swollen beyond further endurance, when the forms of the friendly chief and his wife, bearing upon her shoulders their little visitor, greeted its mother's vision. If there is a mother present who hears my tale, she can tell more perfectly than I can describe, that mother's feelings as she clasped the little one once more to her bosom, and felt its warm heart pulsate to her own. The dress which the child had worn from home had been removed, and in its place its Indian friends had substituted a complete suit of Indian garments, so as completely to metamorphose it into a little squaw. The sequel of this adventure was the establishment of a most ardent attachment and regard on the part of the Indian and his friends for the white settlers. The child, now Mrs. Eells of Missouri, the widow of the late Nathaniel Eells of Whitesboro, still remembers some incidents occurring on the night of her stay in the wigwam, and the kindness of her Indian hostess.

Another anecdote of Judge White, may not be uninteresting in this connection. An Oneida chief, of rather an athletic form, was one day present at his house with a number of his companions, and at length, for amusement, the party commenced wrestling. After a number of trials had been made, the chief came forward and challenged the settler to a clench with him. This was done in a manner, and with a degree of braggadocio, which convinced him, that if he refused to encounter him it would subject him to the constant inconvenience of being brow beaten by an Indian, and cost him the trouble of being believed a coward. In early manhood he had been a wrestler, but he had now become quite corpulent, and for years unused to any athletic feats. He felt conscious, however, of great personal strength, and he concluded, that even should he be thrown, yet as a choice of evils, the being thrown would be a lesser one than the acquiring a character of cowardice by declining. He therefore accepted the challenge and took hold with the Indian, and by a fortunate trip, succeeded almost instantly in throwing him. As he saw him falling, in order to prevent the necessity of ever making another trial of his powers, and of receiving any new challenge, he contrived to fall with all his weight, he then constituting an avoirdupois of some 250 lbs., and as heavily as possible, upon the Indian. The weight, for an instant, drove all breath from the poor fellow's body; and it was some moments before he could get up. At length he slowly arose, shrugged his shoulders with an emphatic - "Ugh! you good fellow, too much!" I need not add, that he was never again challenged to wrestle with an Indian.

I have remarked, that in January, 1785, Judge White brought his whole family from their former home and established them permanently at Whitesboro. In four years after this, he erected the house still standing on the southeastern corner of the village green at Whitesboro, and continued to occupy it until a year or two previous to his death, when he removed to the house owned by him upon the hill, at the junction of the road leading from Whitesboro to Middle Settlement with the road leading from this city past the Burrstone Factory. His death took place at this latter residence, on the 10th of April, in the year 1812. Immediately on the organization of Herkimer county, he was appointed one of its Judges, and held the office until the erection of this county, after which, for many years, he performed the duties of the same office in this county.

I have mentioned that the early settlement of this country was attended with many inconveniences and trials of which it is difficult for us now to form an adequate idea. For the first two years of Judge White's residence at Whitesboro, the nearest mill was situated at Palatine, a distance of about forty miles. This distance too, it must be borne in mind, must be traversed by an Indian path perfectly impassable by any wheeled carriage, and barely permitting a horse to thread his way through it. And I have often heard the early settlers of this county speak of having carried bags of grain upon their backs this distance to be ground, and then returning with the flour in the same manner. In 1786, the mill situated on the Sauquoit, on the road to Whitesboro, now called Wetmore's mill, was erected by him and the late Amos Wetmore. This was the first grist mill in the vicinity.

At the period of his settlement, the agricultural operations of the few inhabitants scattered along the Mohawk valley, from Palatine to the German Flatts, had not revived after the suspension caused by the border war, which had been waged upon them by the war parties of hostile Indians, who were frequently making incursions upon them. And for several years the whole produce of the country was barely sufficient to meet the demand created by Judge White. The want of animal food, for the first year, was severely felt by the settlers. The war had exhausted nearly all the stock of cattle and sheep of the farmers on the Mohawk, and the few that remained were kept with peculiar care for the purpose of increasing the number, and supplying the demand for stocking their farms anew, so as to render domestic animals quite too valuable to be killed for present convenience. During the summer of 1784, the stock of meats brought with them furnished them an abundance, and in the succeeding winter the demand for food had been supplied by the game which was taken; but it was fore-seen that during the next summer, little dependence could be placed upon this resource by men who wished to devote them-selves to the cultivation of the soil. In the spring however, the quantities of pigeons in the woods were so great and so easily taken, as to suggest the idea of preparing a stock of summer pro-visions from them. With this view, they took great numbers of them, and separating the breasts from the remainder of the birds, salted them and laid away one or two barrels of this singular species of food. This answered as an apology for some thing better; and those who ate it declare that, although not so palatable as some delicacies that might be named, yet it tasted nearly as well as the salt that was put upon it, besides carrying the idea of being "actual meat victuals" to boot. These were but a small specimen of a thousand little inconveniences and perplex-ities which the early settlers had to encounter. But they were met and endured with a good nature and a disposition to make the best of their situation, which disarmed them of half their sting. As the settlement of the country went on, they gradually disap-peared, while their memory, for many a year, furnished amuse-ment and satisfaction, and the theme of many a joyous meeting to those who had endured them.

In the year 1786, the settlement of Whitestown had so far increased, that its inhabitants formed a religious society, and employed as a minister, the Reverend Doctor Hillyer, of Orange, New Jersey, and organized the first Presbyterian church which had been formed in the state west of Albany. Whitestown now began to occupy a considerable space in the public eye, and the emigration into this region went on with accelerated velocity. In 1786, a settlement of twenty families was made at Clinton. The next year a number of families planted themselves at New Hartford, and in 1781, churches were organized in both these settlements. In March, 1788, less than four years after the landing of Judge White at the mouth of the Sauquoit Creek, the town of Whitestown was organized, with limits which are rather astounding to the map makers of the present day. Montgomery county, it will be recollected, comprehended all the state west of the then county of Albany. Whitestown was laid off by a line crossing the Mohawk at William Cunningham's house, (a small log cabin which stood at the lower end of Genesee street, upon the site occupied by the Railroad Depot,) and running north and south to the boundaries of the state, and comprehending all the state lying westward, - a territory which, by the census of 1835, was inhabited by more than a million of inhabitants. The first town meeting was held at a barn then owned by Needham Maynard, Esquire, situated on the road leading from Whitesboro to Middle Settlement. I may here remark, that the eastern boundary of Whitestown continued at the same point until the erection of Oneida county eleven years afterwards, when the line was thrown eastward to the present line of the county, in order that the whole of the settlement here might be included in the town of Whitestown. The poll of the first general election for the town was opened at Cayuga, then adjourned to the present village of Salina to receive the votes of some settlers who resided there, thence to Rome, and closed finally at Whitestown. One of the inspectors of this election was the late Erastus Clark, then a resident of Clinton.

During the same year, a treaty was made with the Oneidas by Governor Clinton, William Floyd, Ezra L'Hommedieu, Richard Varick, Samuel Jones, Egbert Benson and Peter Gansevoort, Commissioners acting on behalf of the State, by the terms of which, the nation ceded all their lands to the State, receiving back from it by way of grant, the lands reserved by them for their own purposes, and among other rights, the right of fishing in the waters of Fish Creek and Oneida Lake forever. By this treaty, the actual sovereignty of the Oneidas forever ceased; and instead of remaining an independent nation, exercising their own control over their own territory they became tenants, acknowledging fealty to the state government for the very soil which the God of nature had given them, and which contained the ashes of generations of their fathers. The plea of necessity is made in excuse for many of our dealings with the red men of our country, and perhaps it may in this instance be urged, that the welfare of this then savage tribe demanded that the power of controlling them by the force of the white men's laws should be extended over them. But it cannot be denied, that the operation of the treaty upon their nation could not have been comprehended by the simple and unsuspicious and friendly natives of the forest, when it was proposed to them on the part of the state authorities; and it is mournful to reflect, that in this case, negotiations and the semblance of a fair bargain, has silently been made to work for the Oneidas the same result, which open and unblushing wrong and violation of faith, in view of the nation and the world, has effected for the hapless Cherokees. We should bear this in mind, as we see the miserable and degraded victims of vice, who occasionally visit our streets, bearing the name and inheriting the blood of the countrymen of Sconondoa and Plattcopf - a name that, while it struck with terror, commanded the respect of all who heard it; - blood that the chivalry of the middle ages might have coveted for its characteristics of noble bearing. I say we should bear these facts in mind, and each American should, by his sympathy and his exertions, do all in his power to promote the efforts of those who are engaged in the business of introducing christianity and the arts of civilization among the remnant of the native lords of the whole American soil, who still exist as mere mementos of their former greatness. The dealings of Providence with the whole Indian race, have been very mysterious, and to us, unfathomable. The history of the world furnishes the character of no savage people with so much to admire and so little to disapprove as theirs. While falsehood, treachery, gross impurity and disgusting and soul-enslaving idolatry in its ten thousand forms, have characterized the savage of every other portion of the globe, and have accompanied, in their march through barbarism up to a semi-civilization, the ancinet states of Egypt, Assyria, Greece and Rome, and the various empires of India, Burma and China, verifying the repulsive picture which the great Apostle to the Gentiles gives of man left to the workings of his reprobate mind and uninfluenced by the doctrines of christianity, - the Indian, wherever found uncontaminated by the vices of civilization, exemplifies the virtures of truth, fidelity and chastity, and is found the awe-inspired worshipper of one great, disembodied Spirit, - the creator, governor and father of all things. Yet we have seen the groveling and besotted votaries of Brama, the supporters of the ten thousand deities of Greek and Roman mythology with all its soul-polluting and disgusting orgies, the bloodstained worshippers of the Northern, and the Druidical idolatries, borne with by the hand of Mercy until, upon their benighted minds, a purer light should break to convert them to the true God: while to the poor Indian, the Star of Bethelehem has hitherto but seemed a taper to light him to the grave, - not the day spring from on high to usher in a glorious morning, but the evening star soon, for him, to set in darkness - the blackness of oblivion.

The Oneidas seem destined to follow in the footsteps of the thousands of their red brethren who have disappeared before the march of the white man, like the dew before the risen sun. And there are peculiar features in the circumstances connected with their history which excite a most melancholy, heart-distressing interest. I have remarked, that the Six Nations were distinguished for their noble traits of character above their brethren, even of their own noble race; and the Oneidas were particularly regarded as among the most generous of the confederation consisted of but five nations, the Mohawks, Oneidas, Onondagas, Cayugas and Senecas, and when, after the Tuscaroras, then occupying a portion of Virginia, had been vanquished by the arms of the colonists in 1712, it was concluded to adopt them into the league, the Oneidas gave them a home upon their possession, and at the time of the Rev. Mr. Kirkland's arrival at Oneida, and for several years afterwards, they occupied a territory lying east of Oneida and composing at present a part of the towns of Vernon and Augusta. Subsequently to the war, and previous to the year 1795, they were invited by the Senecas to occupy a portion of their possessions, and took leave of their former abode. In 1787, the Oneidas learning the condition of the Mohegan and Stockbridge Indians, and how they were dwindling from a too near neighborhood to the whites, sent a delegation to invite them to come and make their home with them, and generously ceded to them the use of the lands known as the Brothertown and New Stockbridge tracts, for so long a period as they should choose to occupy them. This was done with the fond hope that here might be a safe resting place for them and their brethren, to grow up together in the knowledge and the arts of civilization. How soon that hope withered! A generation had not passed away - the locks of those who in manhood had welcomed their brethren to their new home had not whitened, before the nation saw itself degraded and polluted with the vices of the white man, and daily sinking and disappearing beneath their influence, with no hope of escape but that

afforded by a removal from the neighborhood of their seductions.
The more thoughtful of the nation, therefore, in the year 1820,
began to look for a new land where they and their children might
gradually acquire the manners and habits of civilized life, away
from the temptations and evil influence of those who, for sordid
and wicked purposes, sought to corrupt them. A purchase was
made by them of a territory at Green Bay, on the west shore of
Lake Michigan, for all who chose to remove thither. The din of
the settler was then unheard within five hundred miles, and they
reasonably hoped, that before the accursed thirst of gain should
have driven our countrymen to the neighborhood of their retreat,
they would have grown up into the early manhood of civilization.
An emigration from the nation at once commenced and has continued from year to year, until few of the enterprising and worthy
remain at the ancient seat of their fathers. But a result which no
fear foretold has befallen them. The white man is again upon
them, - his vices again devastating them, and preparing the way
for a speedy destruction. The home of their adoption, as well as
the home of their fathers, must be bidden farewell, and a new
asylum found in the farther regions of the west. And they are now
preparing, by a removal to a distant territory in Arkansas, to
make one more effort to transmit to their children, with the name
of their fathers, their virtues, and under circumstances which
may afford a hope that their humble beginnings in the arts of
civilization may not be crushed by the approach of the vicious
influences they have twice fled to avoid. That a better fate await
them there, who will not pray? and yet praying, who, in view of
the subject, dare to hope? The spectacle is most mournful. A
people, but yesterday opening its arms to receive the vanquished
to its bosom - to grant an asylum to the hapless and the homeless,
for whom no kindred blood pleaded - cheerfully parting its
possessions to the remnants of races once its enemies, and making
them its brethren and its children; - today separated from its
loved home, as the only means to separate its sons from vice and
annihilation, and occupying a distant and far-off land, - and
preparing tomorrow, as its new home had begun to be associated
with pleasant recollections, to tear itself from it, and seek in the
still farther wilderness, a resting place that should prove an
asylum from the seductions and vices which environed the footsteps of its children. They who had fed and clothed and furnished
pleasant homes to strangers and the oppressed, to become themselves strangers in a strange land, to escape the miserable alterna-

tive of becoming outcasts and a scoff in their own!

In April, 1798, the county of Oneida was erected, comprehending in its boundaries the present counties of Oneida, St. Lawrence, Jefferson, Lewis and Oswego. The first court held after its erection was a court of common pleas, held in the school house near Fort Stanwix, in the town of Rome, on the third Tuesday of May, 1799. The late Jedediah Sanger, of New Hartford, as first judge of the county, presiding, assisted by the late David Ostrom, of this city, and George Huntington, of Rome, judges, and the late Judge Platt acting as clerk. The first circuit court held for Oneida county was held in September of the same year, at the same place, the late Chancellor Lansing, then Chief Justice of the State, presiding. The courts continued to be held at the same school house in Rome until after the December term of the court of common pleas in 1807. At that term, I find an entry setting forth that the court were informed by Charles C. Brodhead, Esquire, sheriff, that the gaol at Whitestown had been completed, and that he had removed the prisoners belonging to the county from Herkimer county gaol, and that they were now confined there. The court thereupon made an order, directing the next session to be held at the school house near the gaol in Whitestown, and from that one-half of the courts of common pleas appear to have been held there, and the remainder at Rome. The circuits were, however, generally held in Whitestown.

In connection with this subject, I have mentioned the name of Jedediah Sanger, and the space he occupied in the early history of the county demands more than a passing notice. Forming a part of the first colony which planted themselves in the village of New Hartford, an active, vigorous and enterprising mind, governed and controlled by unimpeachable integrity, & a high sense of moral obligation, placed him at once in a conspicuous station among the inhabitants of the vicinity. Immediately after his establishment, he erected a grist mill on the site of the present paper mill in the village of New Hartford, then the second mill established in the vicinity. By a judicious and liberal encouragement to emigrants, and particularly mechanics, he succeeded in building up a village, which, for many years, contested the claim of superiority and importance with any of her neighbors. The office of first judge of Oneida county he continued to hold from its organization until the year 1810. He several times occupied a seat in the Legislature, and in the various offices in which he was called to act, served with equal credit to himself and usefulness to the community. To his beneficence the Episcopal Church in New Hartford is indebted for a valuable permanent fund to aid in the support of its minister.

The settlement of Utica commenced at an early period, but was not prosecuted with the vigor that the neighboring settlements were. Whitestown was regarded as the great central point of the whole region up to the years 1793 or 1794. At this period quite a village had grown up there, while Utica, or old Fort Schuyler, as its site was then called, could boast of but three houses. About this time the public attention was directed to Rome, as the probable future metropolis of the State. Its local position favored the idea. It occupied the portage or carrying place between the Mohawk and Wood Creek, which discharging through Oneida Lake into Lake Ontario, formed a channel of communication between the Hudson and the whole chain of western lakes. The connecting the two streams by a navigable canal, which was projected at a very early day, and was accomplished by the Western Inland Lock Navigation Company, which was chartered in 1792, encouraged the belief, that that site must become the focus of the business of the country. And for several years the growth of Rome warranted the expectation. The location of the Seneca turnpike road first operated to change the current of business and divert it to this location. This event took place in the year 1800, and the crossing of the River at this point rendered it immediately important as a place of deposit and of trade. A steady and healthful growth ensued, and the aid and influence of enlightened and enterprising men in the various walks of life, contributed very shortly to render it the leading place of business in the neighborhood. Its present name was given to it in 1798, when it was incorporated as a village, and it has since then continued its municipal capacity until the present day. The first church gathered in this city was organized under the care of the Reverend Bethuel Dodd, as a branch of the church at Whitestown, in the year 1794. The style of the corporation was - "The United Presbyterian Societies of Whitestown and old Fort Schuyler." Previous to that time, although the people of Whitestown had employed a clergyman, the Rev. Dr. Hillyer, whom I have already mentioned, they had not settled a Pastor. Mr. Dodd was ordained Pastor of the United Societies. The union of the two churches continued for more than twenty years under the pastorates of Mr. Dodd and his successor, the Rev. Doctor Carnahan. They were the first Presbyterian churches organized west of the city of Albany, those at Clinton and New Hartford being Congregational in their forms of government. The Episcopal Church in this city was gathered in 1798, and its present church edifice erected in 1803.

I had intended in the present lecture to give detailed notices of a number of persons in the various walks of life, who occupied prominent places in the history of Oneida county; but in looking over my catalogue, I find that anything beyond a simple mention of their names, would occupy quite too large a space for a popular lecture. In taking a survey of the early inhabitants of the county, one cannot fail to be struck with the degree of energy, enterprise, talent and cultivation which characterized the community, and gave a tone and life to the whole fabric of society. Within fifteen years from the day it was one unbroken wilderness, a community sprung up possessing all the constituents which go to form the best regulated states of society. A body of farmers unsurpassed for intelligence, good sense and sterling worth by the agriculturists of any land; a class of merchants active, intelligent, enterprising and an ornament to their calling; a bar learned, dignified, and which shone for years, a brilliant galaxy of talent and erudition; a scientific and highly educated medical faculty, and a clergy that would be a blessing to any land. Without enumerating many who still remain with us, affording us worthy specimens of the generation nearly passed away, and examples for the imitation of the present one, among the names of those who have ceased from their labors, those of Sanger and Risley, of New Hartford, of Bristol and Gridley and Hart, of Paris, of White and Lansing, of Whitestown, of Colt and the Wrights, at Rome, of Mappa and Fisk, of Trenton, and a long list of others which will occur to each person conversant with the county, are sufficient to justify the remark, that the farmers of those days were men of whom we may justly feel an honest pride. And a glance at those who then occupied the place of merchants and physicians, will show that these professions were also filled with no ordinary men. In the profession of law, the names of Gold, and Platt, and Clark, and Williams, and Sill, are alone sufficient to place in the first rank, the character of the bar of any court. And, to revert to the clergy, the memory of the first pastor of the church here and at Whitestown, the Reverend Bethuel Dodd, lives fresh in the memory of all who knew him, and will be transmitted with veneration to their children's children. In this city, also, the Rev. Philander Chase, now the Rt. Rev. Bishop of

Illinois, officiated as an humble missionary, and gathered a little flock, the germ of the Episcopal Church. At New Hartford, the Rev. Dan Bradley, a devoted servant of the Cross, was settled as a pastor in 1791, and continued his care of the church for several years. He was succeeded by the Rev. Mr. Johnson, and in honor of the occasion of his induction to the pastoral office, according to a custom which sounds singular in our ears, but which was introduced from New England, the exercises of the day were con- cluded by an ordination ball. The Rev. Dr. Norton became pastor of the church at Clinton about the year 1792, and continued to officiate in its desk until within the last three or four years, when, yielding to the infirmities of age, he relinquished it. It would be easy to swell the list of names, that our county then boasted, which would be an honor to any community. And while it num- bered among its inhabitants such specimens as I have alluded to, the general tone of its society was characterized by the hospitality which is a peculiar feature of newly settled countries, together with a freedom from the merely artificial usages of life, combined in a remarkable degree with the intellectual cultivation, and the elegancies and accomplishments of the most polished circles. The residents of all parts of the county met and mingled in their social intercourse, and the phrase, "our neighborhood," com- prehended in its limits all the territory within a good day's ride. A horse-back excursion of fifteen miles, over roads which would be deemed impassable by a cavalier of the present day, to pay a visit to a belle, was regarded as a mere bagatelle by the young gentlemen of that period. And the parties, and balls and other merry makings, used to call together all the available constituents of the beau monde from every neighborhood in the vicinity. The fashionables of the present day, might perhaps smile at the style in which the belles were occasionally transported to the place of gathering. A frequent one in the earliest years of the settlement, was the primitive one of riding on horse back en croupe, behind the gallants who invited them. In the state of the roads at that period, travelling on horse back was frequently the only safe or, indeed, practicable method of locomotion, and it was certainly much more sociable and primitive, for the gentleman and lady to ride upon the same horse, while threading a difficult way, than for each one to be all engrossed with the business of guiding a separate animal; and upon the point of delicacy and propriety, possibly as much might be said in favor of sitting upon the same horse, as in the same gig, or upon the same sofa, and perhaps with equal pertinency and justice.

In concluding this lecture, I would remark, that the history of our county is a subject which, while it demands the attention of those of us to whom it is, either by birth or adoption, a home, will richly repay the student for his labors in acquiring a knowledge of it. From the slight glances which I have given of Man and Events connected with it, it will readily appear, that it is a rich mine to him who will explore its recesses. And if my humble endeavors to call your attention to subject shall have contributed to extend a knowledge of those to whom we are indebted for the beautiful and pleasant inheritance we enjoy, and to the means by which it has reached its present state, I shall be amply rewarded for them.

THE EARLY HISTORY OF CLINTON.

A LECTURE.

DELIVERED BEFORE

THE YOUNG MEN'S LYCEUM,

OF

CLINTON.

BY OTHNIEL S. WILLIAMS.

CLINTON:
PUBLISHED BY L. W. PAYNE
1848.

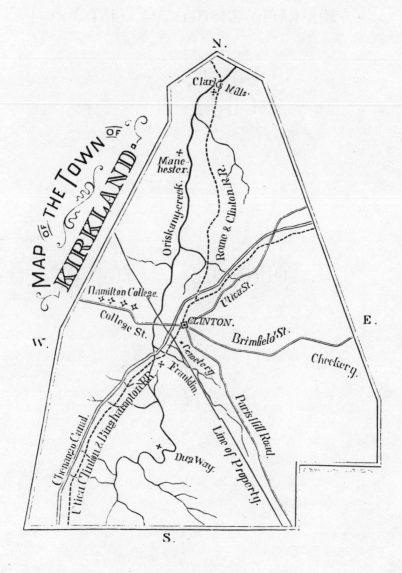

MAP OF THE TOWN OF KIRKLAND.

N.

Clark's Mills.

Manchester.

Oriskany creek.

Rome & Clinton R.R.

Hamilton College.

Utica St.

College St.

CLINTON.

W.

Brimfield St.

E.

Cemetery.

Franklin.

Checkery.

Chenango Canal.

Utica Clinton & Binghamton RR.

Paris Hill Road.

Dug Way.

Line of Property.

S.

The Early History of Clinton

Gentlemen of the Lyceum, and Citizens of Clinton:

I do not propose to offer you this evening a labored address upon the philosophy or the arts of our own, or of ancient days: the sciences I shall not approach, and the mighty deeds of mightier nations and of godlike men will pass unmentioned. I choose a theme far humbler; the gentle or the sterner deeds, the simple hearts and toilworn hands, the hardy labors and the honest lives of our ancestors in these, our present resting places, are all that I can offer.

It may seem a trifling task, a work unworthy of this bustling, railway, plank-road age, to spend our hours in collecting statistics of small settlements or of smaller families; matters of little practical utility when known, and already thickly overspread with the cobwebs of forgetfulness. Be it so; it is sometimes sweet to be idle, to while away an hour in pouring over the legends of the red-man, and the tales of scattered settlers who once were the dwellers here, and perchance too, some century hence, when the vale of the Oriskany shall be but a city and a garden, and there shall be erected here the mansions of grandeur and of power, the homes of the mighty and the honored sons of earth, some worthy descendant of these ancient and noble pioneers may delight to find a memorial of his father's days, a token that he is sprung from earth's noblest lineage.

Previous to the war of the Revolution, a large part of the central and the whole of western New York was an unbroken wilderness. The most western settlements were on the alluvial bottoms of the Mohawk, now known as Herkimer on the north side, and the German Flats on the south side of that river. To this point, German settlers had penetrated at an early day and, faithful to their national character, they dwelt content with their quiet homes and luxuriant harvests, and sought not to penetrate the dark forests and unknown regions beyond them.

True, as early as the old French war, the country had been to some extent, explored. Fort Schuyler had been thrown up on the present site of Utica, and Rome was known as Fort Stanwix. Extensive tracks of land had been granted to favorites of the crown, or to purchasers for a trifling consideration, and some of these tracts had been partially located. Scattered among the Indian tribes might be found the self-denying missionary of the cross, toiling for their welfare, with a fidelity scarcely repaid by the results; and at the crossings of streams and the carrying places of rivers was seen his counterpart, the solitary adventurer for gain, seeking a precarious livelihood, and sometimes perchance, making much gain by driving sharp bargains with the red man. But, the sturdy woodsman was not there, and the Indian and his game roamed over the land unmolested.

The Revolutionary war led our citizens beyond the confines of the German settlements; as soldiers, they penetrated the forests, and with an eye to future habitations, explored the resources of the country. As early as 1766, seven pairs of brothers, from as many different families in the town of Plymouth, in the state of Connecticut, enlisted under the command of Captain David Smith, were marched westward, and during the summer of that year, were stationed by turns at Fort Herkimer, Fort Schuyler, and Fort Stanwix. They visited the surrounding country and at the close of the war, were ready to "go up at once and possess the land."

In the spring of the year 1787, eight families, five of whom were from the same town of Plymouth, after having sojourned for two harvests at German Flats, pushed westward, followed the trail of the "old Moyer road" to what is now Paris Hill, and thence, turning to the north, made their first location of Sunday, the fourth day of March, where is now the village of Clinton. The spot had been visited the fall preceding by Moses Foote, in company with others; and, in the early part of the month of February, 1787, Mr. James Bronson slept for a night on Clinton Green, sheltered from the winter's storm by the upturned roots of a mighty hemlock. Tradition also tells that Ludim Blodget, in the fall of 1786, visited the same spot, and commenced the building of a log-house on the spot where is now the residence of Mrs. Wayne Gridley.

The fact is worthy of remembrance that the exploring party sent out the fall before the settlement, on their journey hither, divided at Paris Hill: a part travelled north until they reached the elevated plain where now stands the dwelling house of Mrs. Baird, and determined upon that as their place of future location. The other party followed the Moyer road westward, until they struck the Oriskany creek, and then wandered down the stream, and at length diverging eastward across the flats and swamps, finally rested upon the dry knoll upon which this village is built. It was not until after much negotiation that the eastern were induced to join the other party, and it required all the shrewdness and rustic eloquence of Moses Foote to prevent a mutiny in his little company.

The names of the eight families who made the settlement, are even now in dispute, and tradition is at fault in giving their history. About five of them, there is no doubt, namely; Moses Foot and his three sons, Bronson Foote, Ira Foot, and Luther Foot, and his son-in-law Barnabas Pond; and the most authentic accounts name the others, Ludim Boldgett, Levi Sherman, and Solomon Hovey. The wife of this Soloman Hovey is said to have been the first white woman who ever stood upon this soil.

Their acknowledged leader was Captain Moses Foot, a man of great energy of character, and well fitted to lead in so untried an enterprise. Habitations were first to be provided; rude huts were soon erected, and Ludim Boldgett finished the house he had commenced the fall before. This was the first regular house; it was the palace of the settlement, though built of logs and covered with leaves and elm bark, and destitute of floors, windows and doors. The other shelters were mere huts built in the simplest manner: crotched sticks were set in the ground, poles were laid in the crotches, and strips of bark were set up against the poles for siding and laid across them for covering. It was quite an object also, to have a hollow bass tree stand in one side of the hut, for that, with a few rude shelves, formed an excellent cupboard and pantry and clothes press.

A street (in name) was laid out, running north and south, and extending from the Royce mansion to the dwelling of Mrs. Hayes; to each family was set apart on that street, a lot of two acres, and on these lots the first houses were built.

During the months of March and April, other families came in, and when spring work commenced, the settlement numbered thirteen families, and by fall that number had increased to about twenty. Soon after the first settlement, and probably during the next season, additional lots were set apart to each family, each containing eight acres, and located adjacent to the two acre lots. As soon as their first rude shelters were provided, the settlers fell zealously to work, girdling and felling trees, and preparing for each, a spot on which to raise a crop of vegetables and Indian corn. In the course of the summer, the place by common consent was called Clinton, in honor of George Clinton who was then Governor of this State.

In the spring of the year 1786, (one year previous to the settlement of this place), Wetmore's Mill was built in Whitestown, about seven miles distant from Clinton, through forests and swamps with only an Indian trail for a path. It was a long day's journey to go to mill and return; and besides the grain must be carried, for the most part, on the shoulders of its owners, for no man in the settlement was opulent enough to own a horse, except Captain Foot; and the sorry jade which he called his own was soon stolen from him by the Indians. In the month of June, 1787, a party of settlers turned out and cleared up a passage for a cart and oxen; and on the next day Mr. Samuel Hubbard drove the first team to Whitestown, and brought back six bushels of corn.

During the same season, Capt. Cassety built a grist mill on the east side of the Oriskany Creek, near the present site of the factory of Barton & Tracy. In September, it was ready for business, and Samuel Hubbard, Salmon Butler and Ludim Blodgett, each shelled a peck of new corn, and the lot falling upon Samuel Hubbard, he carried their joint grist on his back, and furnished the first work for the new mill, which according to practice was ground free of toll. This was the first mill west of German Flats, except that at Whitestown. A saw mill was built the same, or the next season, a little above the grist mill, and on the same dam.

It is gratifying to know that the first settlers early showed a high regard for the institutions of morality and religion. On Sunday the 8th day of April, 1787, the first regular religious meeting was held in Clinton, in the house of Capt. Foot, if that may be called a house, which was merely a pile of logs put up in a cob-house fashion, without floor, chinking or roof. This rude edifice stood on the spot now occupied by the tin-store and the printing office. Moses Foot made the prayer, Barnabas Pond, Bronson Foot and

Ludim Blodgett were the principal singers, and one Caleb Merrills, who had settled near what is now called the Middle Settlement, read a sermon. From that time onward the Sabbath has been duly honored on its return, and with scarcely an interruption, the people have assembled from week to week to join in God's most holy worship.

Thus the first summer rolled away, and fall and winter with their winds and rains and storms approached. The log cabins and the bark huts rising here and there, the little clearings looking out upon the blue sky, and opening earth's bosom to the sun, for the first time for centuries, the blackened stumps and girdled trees showed that the white man had been there; and the yellow pumpkins and the waving corn proved that he had not labored in vain. What in March was a wilderness, gloomy, sad and cheerless, in October began to seem like home; and even with the child and the delicate woman, the longing for New England's rocky hills and happy villages had grown faint and almost vanished before the attractions of this fertile land, and the mutual kindness and hospitality of these dwellers in the wilderness. I hazard nothing in saying that this place has known no days more delightful than its earliest. The eager hope of making a new home, the wild excitement of the forest, the joyous greetings of each other from day to day, that "having all things in common" which kindness, not lawlessness produces, the absence of all envy and strife and separate interest is what the present generation have never known. Witness how kindly, how joyfully the new comer was greeted; how comfortably his family was quartered for the night among the settlers, and treated to the best in the settlement; how all hands turned out in the "gray of the morning" and felled the trees, and piled the logs, and stripped the bark, and covered the new habitation, and filled it with the new comers, before the summer's sun went down. And then what a merry and what an innocent house-warming was there: what eager inquiries about the past and the left-behind, and what bright prospects and promises for the future. True, all this may seem small talk in these days of growth and greatness; yet for simplicity and truth, that was Clinton's golden age, and those were days of happiness, deep and most sincere.

The prospect of the settlement in the spring of the year 1788 were flattering; new settlers came in, and during the season about twenty families were added to the number. When the location was made the year before, it was supposed that the land had never been patented or surveyed, and the settlers intended to appropriate it as the squatters on the western lands now make their claims, to occupy it, improve it, make it home, and when it was offered for sale, to claim a sort of pre-exemption right. As soon however, as they began to explore and clear up the woods, they discovered marked trees, and in the course of the second summer, they ascertained that the whole tract had been granted, by the colony of New York, as early as May 30, 1770 to Daniel Coxe and his associates, and by them had been surveyed and divided into lots. The plot on which the settlement was made was the two thousand and sixteen acres tract, and by this name it is still known by the older inhabitants, and by surveyors. It extends from Daniel P. Northrup's on the east, to the Oriskany creek on the west, and from Solomon Gleason's on the North, to Mrs. Hayes' on the south.

The most curious as well as the most unpleasant part of the discovery they were still to make, and they soon found that this tract had been laid out into twenty lots of equal size, as near as might be, and the proprietors had offered to give the tract to any company of twenty families which would make upon it a permanent settlement. This was favorable, but when the proprietors ascertained that a settlement had already been made, in ignorance of their offer, the motives for making it no longer existed, and they required the settlers to pay for it at the rate of ten shillings per acre. Accordingly in the summer of 1788, Capt. Foot was sent to Philadelphia to transact the business, and contracts were made for the purchase of the whole tract, which in time were consummated, and the several lots taken up by the different settlers. The present site of the village was a triangular piece called the handkerchief lot, from its resemblance to a half handkerchief, and was bought by Capt. Foot.

Death did not forget the settlement in the wilderness. In the spring of this year, Merab Tuttle, a daughter of Col. Timothy Tuttle, about 17 years of age, in company with Anna Foot, a daughter of Moses Foot, was returning just at sundown from a visit at William Cook's, who then lived on the farm now owned by Mr. Lucas. They reached the Oriskany, its banks were filled with the spring floods, and its waters were dark and threatening. No bridge, as now, promised safety to the crossing traveller; two logs, felled by the woodsman's axe, furnished the only passage over the stream. They feared, they hesitated, but at length went forward, Miss Foot leading the way; when about one half of the distance was gone over, she heard a shriek, and turning, she saw her companion just plunging beneath the waters. The instant and faithful search that was made availed not: she perished, and her corpse was found the next day, left by the subsiding waters, on the bank of the stream, near the present site of Clinton Factory. That night there was sadness in many habitations, and great was the mourning at her burial. One of their loveliest daughters was snatched away; the delight of many had departed; and the simple hearted grief of our fathers and mothers puts to shame the parade of mourning, and the hollowness of heart which mark many a modern funeral. Her grave was first dug on "the Green", but that spot being then thought too wet, she was finally buried in the south part of the present burying ground, which was then a part of her father's farm.

It is worthy of remark that there was little sickness among the settlers; very few of those diseases which now make a removal to a new country so fearful, were known, and deaths occurred only at rare intervals. The second death was that of Thos. Fancher, Jr., who was killed by a falling tree in 1791; and the third was that of Mrs. Mercy Stebbins, who died in 1792 at the age of 26 years. She was the wife of Judah Stebbins, Jun., and the mother of James D. Stebbins.

Marrying and giving in marriage were among the incidents of those days; and on the same day in 1788, Elias Dewey was wedded to Anna Foot, and Andrew Blanchard took to wife, Mary Cook. It is said that the first public wedding in the settlement took place this year. Mr. Leverett and Miss Cheesebro, (a sister of Mrs. Benedict Babcock, sen.) were the parties, and the party met in a log house which formerly stood on a knoll in the orchard east of the Congden house. Jason Parker of Utica, was among the invited guests; it was a merry time, and though the fare was rustic, the company was full of rejoicing.

Many settlers arrived in 1789; among others, Jesse Curtiss, Esq., who still remains with us, having arrived at a good old age, most honored and beloved. He came from Utica in the spring, and brought on his back, from the log huts at that place, a skippel (three pecks) of seed wheat. It is no disparagement to his descendants to express a doubt whether, with all their very commendable zeal for agricultural societies and farmers' clubs, they would be willing to carry their Italian or Siberian seed, half as far on their shoulders, as did their worthy father.

It is said, (though of this there is some doubt,) that horses were seen this year in the settlement for the first time, if we except the one stolen from Captain Foot by the Indians. William Carpenter and Nathan Marsh each had one, and during the fall they went to Albany on horseback. Perhaps I should mention, by way of comparing old roads with modern ones, that Jesse Curtiss and Bartholemew Pond started on foot at the same time, and arrived at Albany some hours before them.

During the summer of this year, the people were reduced to great straits for bread. The flour, of which they rarely tasted, was gone; their corn and meal were almost exhausted; the last year's crop of potatoes was consumed; and the new crop was not matured. Even at planting time, their supply was so small, that the eyes of the potatoes were cut out and planted, and the residue used for food; the few cattle they possessed were too useful and too valuable to be killed, except in the greatest extremity, and famine verily stared them in the face. And bear in mind, they had not money to use as freely as we may have, in these later days. I do not suppose there were five dollars in the whole community, and the nearest places of supply were quite remote. Many searched the earth for ground nuts, and roots and leeks; the streams were frequented for fish and the forest for game; and most lucky was that man who could rob the bear of her whelps, or perchance destroy the mother and her cubs together. All this answered not; children cried from hunger; man denied himself to feed the weak and the helpless, and something must be done. Think, Oh think, for a moment, ye who now dwell in comfort and wealth, and plenty, in these valleys, and on these hill sides, that less than sixty years ago, in these very places, your fathers and mothers hungered for bread!

A small party went to Fort Plain in Montgomery county, and represented the destitute condition of the people to a farmer and miller by the name of Isaac Paris, and earnestly appealed to him for assistance. He answered their appeal with a readiness and a fullness which did honor to his heart; he loaded a small flat-boat with flour and meal, and sent it up the Mohawk, as far as the mouth of the Oriskany. There it was met by a company of our fathers, re-shipped into a log canoe, dug out by their own hands, and thence they paddled and drew it up the creek, as far as the site of the bridge near the Clinton factory, and from that landing, the cargo was transported in carts to the village. With what gladness and rejoicing was that cargo received, and what shouting was heard on its arrival. Grand was the celebration and loud was the rejoicing when the first boat passed from the Hudson to the Lakes; the gladness was deeper, the joy was more entirely from the heart, when the first canoe in the hands of the white man came up the Oriskany, laden as it were, with hope and life to them, and their wives and their little ones.

And what think you was the payment Mr. Paris agreed to receive? For the whole transaction had on one side a face of business. Nothing less than Ginseng roots, to be delivered to him the next fall. This plant, now so rarely found in this vicinity, in those days grew in great abundance: it was sold to traders, sent to our seaports, and thence shipped to Europe, where it was for a long time regarded as an antidote to the plague.

The name of Paris was not forgotten, and in 1792, when a town was set off from Whitestown, Clinton, which was the largest settlement within its limits, gave to it the name of its benefactor.

The settlers this year began to erect for themselves more permanent habitations. Col. Timothy Tuttle built the first frame house, and a part of it still remains, and forms the carriage house on the late residence of Samuel Royce.

Ebenezer Butler, Jr.; the same year built the second frame house on the spot where is now the residence of Mr. Asa Olmstead, and there he opened and kept the first store in town.

About the 20th day of October, 1789, the snow fell to the depth of nearly two feet, upon a bed of mud not much less; the weather became severely cold and inclement, and most forbidding to the wayfarer and laborer. Precisely at this time, a settler, zealous to build a new frame house before the winter should set in with its full severity, went to Captain Cassety's saw mill, and for three days and two nights, alone, and without rest or intermission, continued to saw the lumber necessary for the building. When the task was ended, his hands were glazed, as if by fire, from using so constantly the cold iron bars of the saw mill; he felt himself well repaid, however, for all his toil and fatigue, for in a few days he reared a frame dwelling sixteen feet square. That dwelling is now the kitchen of Mr. Horatio Curtiss, and that diligent settler was Jesse Curtiss, already mentioned.

The first-born child in the village was Clinton Foot, a son of Luther Foot, who died before he arrived at manhood. The second born child is still living, and in our midst; and whom reckon you she is? None other than Mrs. Fanny Gridley, the wife of our honored townsman, Orrin Gridley.

Julius Pond, now deceased, was the third child, being born July

26, 1789; and the fourth was James D. Stebbins, who was born on the 11th day of Sept. 1790.

The settlement continued to increase from year to year, and to extend farther and farther from the centre, and before the year 1793, most of the farms within two miles of the village, and many beyond that distance, were bought by actual settlers, and clearings on them commenced.

In the year 1792, Thomas Hart removed here, the ancestor of a family which have been, and are now, much distinguished in this State; and he, with one Seth Roberts, opened a store in the building where Ebenezer Butler had traded before.

In the year 1793, Judah Stebbins built the first two-story house; this house still stands, being the large yellow dwelling on the farm of Mr. Edwin J. Stebbins, his grandson. The large barn on the same farm is the oldest in the vicinity, having been built in 1789, and during the latter part of the same season, the large barn on the farm of Rev. Hiram H. Kellogg, was built. A single fact shows at once the necessities and the laborious habits of those days; the clapboards on this dwelling-house were rived or split out of pine trees, by Mr. Stebbins' own hands. Now, the builder is hardly content with the best of sawed half-inch, delivered at his door.

Sometimes our fathers met with odd adventures. The bear in those days was a nuisance, being destruction to green corn and certain death to young pigs. I will not go into particulars about the farmer in a neighboring settlement, who, after feeding his drove of hogs from the cornfield, in counting them over the fence, found that a bear had added himself to the number, nor the alarm among the porkers, when the unwelcome guest was discovered. Suffice it to say, with native instinct they straight-way formed themselves into a circle, with their noses turned outwards, and thus made a stout and successful resistance.

In the fall of 1790, Mr. Curtiss, and three or four others, were returning from meeting on Sunday afternoon, and their path led through a cornfield near where Mr. Gunn now lives. They heard an unusual rustling in the corn and in searching for the cause, soon discovered two bear cubs busily engaged in breaking down and destroying the ripening corn. Forthwith they set upon them, and despite their grunts and cries, by dint of blows and kicks, soon dispatched them. The same afternoon, Mr. Bronson, on returning home from meeting, found the old bear sitting very quietly on the steps of his door, little dreaming of the sad calamity which had even then overtaken her children.

The early settlers were wholly from New England, and for many years almost entirely from the States of Connecticut and Massachusetts. Its whole history shows the striking influence of early habits and education; for from 1787, to the present day, the place has continued to possess many of the marks of a New England town. The prevailing morality, the staid habits, and the attachment to education, which are found on all sides, bespeak, beyond a doubt, our Eastern and our Puritan origin - a descent I trust we may never be ashamed to own, and shall always strive to honor.

The street leading past the house of James D. Stebbins, was for a long time called Brimfield street, being settled entirely by immigrants from Brimfield, in Massachusetts. Speaking of names brings to mind several which came early into use, and are not yet forgotten. The street leading to Utica for many years was known as Toggletown, from the straight post-and-board fence, which was then very common. Even to this day, some of the old inhabitants speak of that street as Toggletown.

The name of Chuckery is indelibly impressed upon the eastern part of the town, and it has been handed down to a second generation of settlements, for a gathering of houses in the town of Fenner, Madison county, which was settled by a swarming from the parent hive, is to this day called New Chuckery. The modern designation is Perryville. As the story goes, (I vouch not for its truth,) the name came in this wise: In Massachusetts, according to established custom, the Governor, many years ago, published the usual proclamation for the annual Thanksgiving, which was to be read in all the Churches. Then, as now, in appropriate terms he called upon the people to render a tribute of gratitude, for the blessings of Providence upon their farms, their fisheries and their merchandise. In Egrement, some mischievous wag possessing himself of the copy which the clergyman had prepared to read to the congregation the next Sabbath, changed the word fisheries to Chuckeries; and so the unsuspecting pastor read it to the no small edification of his congregation. Soon after, a company of colonists from that town came westward, and settling here, gave this odd name to their resting place.

Some account has already been given to the first religious meeting held in the village; but there was not any minister in the place till the month of November, 1788, when the Rev. Samuel Ells, then Pastor of the Congregational Church in Branford, Connecticut, visited the place, tarried sometime, preached, and baptized one adult and twenty-two children. He also formed a covenant, which much resembled the half-way covenant, so popular in those days in New England, and this was signed by nine males and seven females. This covenant was not very fully orthodox in its character, inasmuch as it required merely moral character, historic faith and baptism, but not saving faith or communion, but doubtless was much better than the absence of all religious associations.

In August, 1791, Dr. Edwards, better known as the younger Edwards, then Pastor of a Church in New Haven, Conn., arrived here and organized a Church, (the half-way covenant having been abandoned) consisting of about thirty members.

On the 26th day of September, 1791, "The Society of Clinton" was organized by the election of Moses Foot, Eli Bristol, Ebenezer Butler, Jun., Hannaniah Ellinwood, Ebenezer and Samuel Tuttle as Trustees. The articles of association are dated September 1st, 1791, and were signed by eighty-three members, and embraced nearly all the prominent men of the settlement.

The next year, the Rev. Asahel S. Norton "came at the request of the people to preach the Gospel of Salvation", and having been invited to become the Pastor of the Church and Society, he was ordained to the work of the Gospel Ministry, and duly installed the Pastor of this people on the 18th day of Sept., 1793, in the open air and on the centre of Clinton Green. His salary was fixed at three hundred and thirty-three and a third dollars; and he continued without interruption as the pastor for forty years, when he was dismissed at his own urgent request. He still dwells on the farm which has been his home for more than half a century, and though his eye has become dim, his natural strength has not abated; he lives, full of faith and goodness, beloved and venerated by all, as one of the fathers of the land.

The first meeting house was a log building, erected on the Green in 1792. This was used till 1796, when the old white meeting house was built on the same spot. While this building was in progress, the schoolhouse, a wooden building which occupied the site of the old brick schoolhouse, was occupied as a place of worship. That schoolhouse was removed in 1795, to make more room for the brick one, and now is tenanted by Mr. Slocum, as a dwelling house. As is well-known, the white meeting house was torn down; its materials used in building the present schoolhouse, and the present stone Church was erected instead thereof.

For many years, the Congregational was the only Society, and nearly all the population attended its meetings and contributed to its support. As the population increased, however, diversity of opinions began to prevail; the articles of other denominations obtained a foothold with some, and total or partial unbelief with others.

As early as 1776, the Rev. Samuel Kirkland dwelt as a missionary among the Oneida Indians, and labored with much zeal and some success to lead them in the paths of peace. By the war of the Revolution, his labors were somewhat interrupted; he removed his family to New England, but still continued himself among the Indians, and it was mainly owing to his efforts that the Oneidas, as a tribe, continued the faithful friends of the colonists. He acted for a time as chaplain in the American army; accompanied the expedition of General Sullivan against the hostile Iroquois in 1779 and by his experience and adivce, rendered great service to the country. So sensible indeed was government of the value of his services, that in the year 1789, the tract well-known as Kirkland's Patent, was granted to him by the Legislature of this State. This patent was two miles square, and lies on the west side of the Property Line, its northeast corner being near the North College. The Property Line was established by a treaty between the State of New York and the Oneida Indians, by which the latter ceded to the former all their lands lying north and east of that line. It extended from the head waters of the Unadilla River to Wood Creek, its course being North 27° East, and forms the western boundary of Coxe's patent. A person standing on College Hill in a clear day, can easily trace this famous boundary southward and eastward from the corner of Kirkland's Patent, opposite the North College, crossing the road obliquely above the schoolhouse at the foot of the hill, passing through Noel Foot's saw mill and dwelling house, following the road leading past the residence of Eurotas Hart, and thence stretching away south of Paris Hill to its termination in the town of Bridgewater.

Mr. Kirkland removed to his patent in 1789, and from that time to his death, which occurred on the 28th day of March, 1808, he dwelt on his beautiful domain. About the year 1791, he built, and afterwards occupied a small frame house, which, until recently, stood in the centre of the meadow, south of Mr. Nelson's, and in 1795, he erected the present family mansion. He was a noble man, the friend of his race, both red man and white, and a long line of good deeds proclaim his zeal and liberality in promoting the interests of learning and religion. Before he settled on his newly acquired territory, he had conceived and cherished the plan of founding thereon a school where the white and the red man's sons might meet and mingle together, and with mutual emulation, stimulate each other in the pursuits of learning.

In 1792, he gave a liberal endowment of land for the purpose of founding such a school, and in 1793, "Hamilton Oneida Academy" was incorporated, and the next year the academic and collegiate building, known as Oneida Hall, was erected, partially finished, and the school commenced under the instruction of the Rev. John Niles.

I find among the contributors to the funds of this infant college, the name of almost every settler then residing in this vicinity, showing the entire union of heart and hand which prevailed and their great good will toward this enterprise. The school prospered year by year; and it received the kind protection and fostering care of its founder, who several times during his life gave it very considerable endowments, and even in his death, did not forget it. This academy was for many years the most noted seat of learning in the central and western part of the state, and its rolls contain the names of many men who have since been distinguished in Western New York. Few Indians, however, tarried long within its walls; the chase and the hunting-ground, and I fear, the fire water had for them more attractions.

On the 26th Day of May, 1812, it was chartered; by the Regents of the University, as Hamilton College, and since that day, with some painful and occasional interruptions, it has been growing with our people's growth until, at length, by public munificence and private liberality, it has struck deep its roots, and spread wide its branches over all this middle land.

Time forbids at present to give a more detailed history of this institution, but I trust that ere long, some gifted son of Hamilton, warmed with filial fire, will give to the world the record of her birth and infancy, and maturer years; the story of her trials and her victories, too; the literary lineage of her sons, her Parker, her Robinson and her Barnes; her Kirklands, her Gridleys and her Smiths.

The early founding of Hamilton Oneida Academy and its subsequent growth, have impressed a marked character upon the people. They have ever been the patrons of learning in all its grades; and a good name has Clinton gained through the land by its halls of learning. Other schools have sprung up, and "The Female Seminary", "Clinton Grammer School", "The Clinton

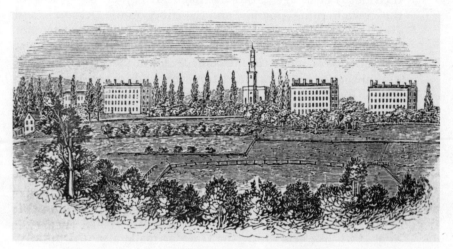

Barber & Howe Historical Collections

Hamilton College, Clinton

Liberal Institute", and "The Ladies' Seminary", have each in its appropriate department rendered good service in the common cause.

When the first settlements were made in Central New York, the Indian abounded in all this region, and the far-famed and much feared Iroquois were sovereigns in the land. Their prowess and their deeds of savage daring extended far beyond the bounds of their own hunting grounds, and the tribes on the Delaware, and even the distant south, had learned to dread the war-whoop of the resolute Oneida and the ferocious Mohawk. The Oneida was first among his equals, in the confederacy of the six nations, and his hunting grounds extended from the lands of the Mohawk, to that of the Onondaga, and far away toward the south, into the State of Pennsylvania.

A powerful and noble tribe, they were also generous, and about the period of the revolution, they granted to the Stockbridge Indians of Mass., a tract of land, and invited this tribe, then sorely pressed on all sides by the white man, to leave their home and again to dwell in the wilderness. They came and occupied the territory called Stockbridge, until the far west beckoned them away, and they departed towards the setting sun. Soon after, with like generosity, the Oneidas made a similar grant to several other decayed New England nations, and in that medley of tribes called the Brothertown Indians, we had in our midst the last remnants of the noble Mohegan, immortalized by the novelist, the fierce Narraganset, and the wily Pequot, so noted in early New England annals, and so fiercely fought by our quiet Puritan fathers. How sad and how miserable a termination of the lineage of the mighty King Philip, of Mount Hope! Yet in the last fitful twilight of the race, a manly form is seen, a noble life is shown - Asa Dick was a Narraganset!

In the quiet rambles of the Oneidas over their own hunting grounds, the vale of the Oriskany, the "valley of nettles", and the sloping hills on either side, were favorite places of resort; and after this settlement was commenced, they were its constant visitors. It is very common, and well enough too, to eulogize the Indian character in general, but when we come to speak of specific acts, we shall often find that opportunity produced covetousness, and covetousness was followed by stealing and its attendant vices. The story of the "fine fat steer", so often told, furnishes of this a good illustration. That story I will briefly tell, as I have the facts from an eye witness and a party to the transaction.

In 1787, Theodore Manross, who had commenced a clearing on the farm for many years occupied by Jesse Wood, missed from his herd a fine fat steer. Suspicion soon fell upon a party of Oneidas, who, lead by a chief called Beechtree, had for some days been encamped on the hill a little south of him, and were digging ginseng in the vicinity; search was made, their encampment was deserted, and the fresh offals of the animal were found near by, secreted.

A party of ten or twelve active and resolute young men were soon formed. Moses Foot was their captain, and among the company were Jesse Curtiss, Levi Barker, and several other familiar names.

The Indian trail was fresh and their path through the nettles and undergrowth was as plain to the sharp eyes of the eager pursuers, as a beaten track to the traveller. They followed them to Paris Hill, thence to the Sauquoit, a little north of the present village, and thence down the stream. As they came near New Hartford, the track was so fresh that it was manifest they were close upon the Indians. Soon they spied them marching single file, and taking a little circuit, they came into their path before them, and turning towards them, met them face to face.

"Stop!" said Captain Foot, to Beechtree, their leader, "you have stolen and killed the white man's steer".

"Indian has not killed the white man's steer," replied Beechtree, leaping forward and drawing from his belt his long hunting knife. Quick as thought, Captain Foot raised a heavy cane and brought it down with convincing force upon the crown of the naked head of Beechtree. He winced and settled down beneath the powerful blow; it was enough, the party surrendered, and on search being made the hide and bell of the missing animal was found in the pack of one of the Indians, who bore the expressive cognomen of "Saucy Nick".

This was pretty good proof. As the modern and fashionable defenses of sleep walking, insanity and the like were not known to these untutored wild ones, they frankly confessed the deed. The prisoners were marched back in a body and forthwith were confined and guarded in the house of Col. Timothy Tuttle, standing on the present site of the Royce mansion. Mr. Kirkland was immediately sent for, and by permission of the guard, they sent a swift messenger to Oneida to summon their friends and chiefs to their assistance, sending the message to them at the same time, to drive over a certain cow as a means of settlement for the wrong committed.

Before the morning sun had risen high, their friends appeared, led by the wise and venerable Skenandoa, Mr. Kirkland acting as interpreter. And finally it was agreed that the Indians should give the cow, which had been driven from Oneida, to Mr. Manross, to make him good, and the ginseng which they had dug, to the party of young men who had pursued them, to pay them for their time and trouble. The whole matter was concluded before noon, and this resolute conduct of the settlers entirely prevented the recurrence of similar aggressions.

"Saucy Nick" was alone, sullen and revengeful. The theft was more especially charged to and proved upon him; and on the march from New Hartford to Clinton, he had had a bitter wrangle with one Lemuel Cook, who, if all accounts are true, was as much entitled to the appellation of "saucy", as Nick himself. His foul and abusive speech had sunk deep into the Indian's memory, and his ardent longing was for revenge and blood. Soon after he unsuccessfully attempted to kill Cook at Fort Schuyler, and the next season as Cook was ploughing on his farm, (being the farm owned for many years by Mr. Pollard) an Indian arrow whistled swiftly past his ear. The hand that sent it, though unseen, could not be mistaken, and Cook, warned of his danger, soon sold his farm and returned to Connecticut.

The family of "Saucy Nick" was much noted among the Oneidas, and for many years, dwelt at Oneida Castle. Of powerful frames, and fierce and vindictive temper, they were feared and hated. The Rev. Samuel Kirkland, while he lived at Oneida, before the revolution, saved his life from the fury of one of this family, by being concealed and locked up by his friends in a chest of drawers. The character of this family is well drawn by Cooper, in his "Hunted Knoll," and doubtless "Saucy Nick", sat for the picture of Wyandotte, though as to his tribe and age and adventures, the writer has used the license of the novelist.

Many of the Oneidas were men of much ability and nobleness of character. The eloquence of the great Skenandoa is in the mouth of every schoolboy; and the exalted character which he maintained for half a century, should be held in undying remembrance. His steadfast affection for his teacher, Mr. Kirkland, and through him for the white man, was a wonderful feature in his character, and was only surpassed by his deep love and veneration for his still greater Teacher above. After a century of years had rolled over his head, he often came to Clinton to die, and although in this leading object of his wishes, he was not gratified, yet his body, after his decease, was brought here by his mourning tribe, and now he rests in peace by the side of his teacher, ready to use his own expressive wish, "to go up with him at the great resurrection."

Priest Occum was a Stockbridge, an educated clergyman, and preached with much success. He went to England and preached in the presence of King George the 3rd, with great applause, and before leaving the realm, the King gave him a library. It is a curious fact that he was the officiating clergyman at the first marriage of our much esteemed and recently departed townsman, William Stebbins.

Elijah Wampe was a Nehantic, from Farmington, and made a settlement on the grant from the Oneidas early in the revolution. When the tories made that most desolating attack upon Cherry Valley and the adjacent settlements, a body of about four hundred Indians, led on by twenty tories, came from the west, and on their march, stopped at Wampe's opening. He was the only New England Indian who remained on the grant, the others having through fear returned to their old haunts, or stopped among the settlements on the Mohawk. The description of this war party from the lips of this worthy and faithful and earnest old Indian, must have been touching in the extreme. They behaved very well when going east, but on their return they stopped again, elated by victory and made ferocious by rum; decked in all their war attire, laden with the trophies of their savage deeds, and bearing upon poles, the bloody scalps of the white settlers, they were indeed a fearful company. The old man said, with flashing eyes as he told the story, "Wampe keep still, but his blood boiled to see the wretches." He, however, treated them to his best, and as they were leaving, they told him that they must have two fat hogs, and if he would give so much, they would not molest him or his property. He did so, and the villains, as they passed along, shot down and carried off two of his cows. Wampe, in terror, fled and took refuge with the garrison at Fort Stanwix.

These sketches must be brought to a close. Many things remain untold: the amusing anecdote, the personal adventure and the external changes of our village have been but slightly touched upon. Our fathers laid broad and deep the foundations of many useful institutions, and they have delivered a good work to the present generation. Let ours be the duty to prosecute it, and no laborer shall depart unpaid. The lover of money shall reap a rich

reward in his increasing gains, and the friend of virtue and
science a higher reward in his inward satisfaction.

————————

HON. O.S. WILLIAMS,
  Dear Sir: The undersigned solicit for publication a copy of the
Lecture delivered by you, last evening, before the "Young Men's
Lyceum," on "The Early History of Clinton." Be acceding to this
request, and thus permitting the many interesting facts embodied
in your address to receive a more permanent and available form,
you will greatly oblige those who were present, as well as many
who were unable to be present at its delivery.

Yours very sincerely,

C.C. COOK,	O. GRIDLEY,
P. FAKE,	H.G. EVERETT,
EDWARD NORTH,	ELI B. LUCAS,
HORATIO CURTISS,	EDWARD MANNERING,
R. ROOT,	C. BARROWS,
ROB'T. G. VERMILYE.	

Clinton, February 25, 1847.

PUBLICATIONS

OF THE

ONEIDA HISTORICAL SOCIETY AT UTICA

No. 5

Second Annual Address

BEFORE THE SOCIETY

BY

WILLIAM TRACY

OF NEW YORK

January 13th 1880

William S. Gottsberger, Printer, New York.

Second Annual Address Before the Oneida Historical Society

Within the last forty years, the earlier history of Oneida County has been examined and illustrated by the pens of several of your distinguished fellow citizens. When I read here, "Notice of men and events connected with the early history of Oneida County", I think no one had attempted any written contributions to it. Since then, quite a number of your citizens have supplemented what I then attempted. My friend, Judge Pomeroy Jones, had given full and valuable annals of each of its towns with notices of their settlers. Judge Othniel S. Williams has collected the traditions of the settlement of Kirkland. Mr. John F. Seymour[1] has made a very interesting addition to your history in his address at Trenton. David E. Wager, Esquire has written valuable and interesting notices of Rome. Doctor M. M. Bagg, an exhaustive work upon the history of this city, and my early and valued friend, Judge William J. Bacon,[2] in his address on the members of the bar of this county, has left little to be added to the subject. You would not thank me for a fresh recital of their historical sketches. I shall not, therefore, attempt a review of the history of Oneida County, but will confine myself to a comparative view of what she was in her early stages while the hand of improvement was attacking her forests to convert them into farms, and the homes of civilized life

---

[1] John F. Seymour "Centennial Address July 4, 1876, Trenton, N.Y." pp. 535-540, Samuel W. Durant, *History of Oneida County, New York 1667-1878*, Everts & Fariss, 1878.

[2] William J. Bacon "The Early Bar of Oneida County." pp. 206-216, Durant, op. cit.

and what she has become under the plastic hand of the emigrants and their sons and daughters with incidental anecdotes of a few of its inhabitants.

In 1785, the region, now covered with beautiful farms and villages, and the two manufacturing and commercial cities, Utica and Rome, now constituting this County, was a wilderness. The only land which had been denuded of its forest consisted of two small Indian clearings at Oriskany and Oneida Castle. An Indian village occupied the left bank of the Oriskany creek just eastward of the site of the woolen factory which was built as early as 1810. Another Indian village at Oneida Castle was the principal home of the tribe which gave to it its name. During the year first mentioned, the late Judge Hugh White, with a family consisting of several sons and daughters, emigrated from Middletown, Connecticut and established himself in the present village of Whitesboro, building a log house on the southern extremity of the village green. His settlement gave the name of Whitestown and of the Whitestown Country to the lands lying westward of the German flats and northward to the boundaries of the State. He was soon followed by numbers of emigrants chiefly from Connecticut and Massachusetts, though there were some from the other settlements of this State and some from New Jersey. Many of them had been soldiers in the Revolutionary Army. Thirty six years after this period it became necessary for pensioners under the Act of Congress of 1818 to appear before the county courts and make depositions as to their services. In Oneida County, the Court appointed a day to hear their applications. There then appeared a few less than two hundred of these veterans. After having made their depositions, they formed into line and, led by a Revolutionary drummer, marched through the streets and around the village green. As the youngest Revolutionary soldier must then have been about fifty years old, it is probable that an equal number of those who had settled in Oneida County had, within the thirty six years after the war, died and that there may have been four or five hundred soldiers who had emigrated to Oneida County, or a sufficient number to constitute a battalion. I will here remark that among the officers of the Army who became inhabitants of the County were General Frederick William Augustus, Baron Steuben, who died at his residence in Steuben in 1794, General William Floyd, one of the signers of the Declaration of Independence, Colonel Benjamin Walker, who had been aid to Washington and subsequently to Baron Steuben. He

Rome Historical Society

Baron Steuben (1730-1794)

became an inhabitant of Utica and died here; and Colonel Garret G. Lansing of Oriskany. The latter once told me the story of his becoming a soldier. His father resided in Albany. A week before Garret became sixteen years old, the age required for military service, he overheard his mother tell his father that Garry would become of age for being enrolled during the next week and it would be prudent to say nothing of it. The boy was determined to become a soldier and no sooner had he heard the news that he might be a subject of enrollment, than he went to the enrolling officer and told him his age. He was enrolled and the next week started with a small detachment of new militia men to reach the northern Army. This reached Fort Edward when the funeral services over the remains of Miss McCrea had just been commenced. After her burial, the detachment marched onward toward the rear of the Army. Before they came up to it, it was ordered to make a detour away from their line which, it was supposed, could be accomplished during the day. Their commissariat consisted of a single piece of pork, sufficient to last them until they should reach their comrades. This was placed in a pot and set upon a fire, and as the boy of the party, young Lansing was installed cook and left alone to watch the fire. After regarding the pot attentively for an hour or two with nothing to amuse him, he fell asleep and awoke to see a bear, which had been attracted by the savory mess, running off with the pork. He had obtained it by upsetting the kettle from the fire and capturing the contents. Young Lansing was confounded and it required a very little flight of imagination to present to his minds eye the picture of his hungry companions when they should return and find their pork gone through his neglect. He, therefore concluded, rather than meet them, to avail himself of a hiding place where he could remain until their anger should subside. The party came back and found the contents of the pot missing and, seeing nothing of their cook, concluded that he had been killed by the Indians and their pork consumed by them. But when he turned up, their joy at his being alive overcame their disappointment. He completed a short term of service and, at its close, was made an ensign in the regular Army and remained in the Army until the close of the war. The reason of his settling at Oriskany is perhaps worthy of note.

When quite a lad, he had accompanied a surveying party up the Mohawk. At the mouth of Oriskany Creek it landed and found the Indians of the village engaged in a dance. He was struck with the beauty of the clearing with its surrounding forest. Often after he left the Army, this scene was recalled to him and, after a few years spent in Washington County, the memory of the spot led him to visit it and purchase a farm there and erect a house in which he spent the residue of his life. He died in 1831, respected and beloved by all who knew him.

At the time Judge White arrived in this County, with the exception of the clearings at Oriskany and Oneida, there was absolutely no land ready for cultivation, and no roads. Before the Revolutionary War, there were Indian foot paths leading from Oneida to Fort Stanwix, and again from that point along the Mohawk to the German Flats, and again from Oneida through the present towns of Vernon and Westmoreland to Fort Schuyler. There were no other roads, and these would not have admitted horseback riders. The troops, which, during the French War in 1758, passed up to Fort Stanwix, were forced to cut paths for their passage; but, they had overgrown and during the Revolutionary War they had again to be cut anew, but they had left no roads. Judge White came up the river in a boat from Schenectady with his family and goods and landed them at the mouth of the Sauquoit, which for several years after, continued to be the usual landing place of the small boats which navigated the river. The territory then presented a very different scene from the one which now greets the observer - very different from that which greets the emigrant to the new lands in the western and southwestern States. There the settler finds a soil ready for his plough; here no prairie met the vision of the former. Everywhere was unbroken heavily timbered forest to be subdued only by the joint efforts of the axeman and cultivator. Severe toil was required to clear and fence and prepare the soil for the agriculturist. It was literally the abode of only wild beasts and redmen, whose living was obtained from the chase. There was no mill nearer than Palatine and, for two or three years, the emigrant had to carry his grain upon his back for forty miles to be ground, or crush it in a primitive mortar made by burning a cavity in a log of wood. No house of worship, nearer than the German Flats, invited the emigrant from the land of the Pilgrims and their churches to worship the God of their fathers. His task was to convert this territory into a fit abode for more than two hundred thousand people who now occupy it, covered with farms and homesteads and villages and cities, adorned with churches, schools and institutions of benevolence and taste. Within the limits of less than a single century this has been done, and the wilderness has blossomed as the rose.

Within five years from the time Judge White planted his footsteps on the bank of the Sauquoit, the work had been well begun.
Light had been made to penetrate the forest, farms had been
partly cleared, and emigrants had established themselves in comfortable homesteads along the valleys of the Mohawk, the Sauquoit, and the Oriskany; highways had been opened from settlement to settlement. Whitesboro, Rome and Clinton had become
small villages. Utica, under the name of Old Fort Schuyler, was
still, and for several years after, but a small hamlet with only a
blacksmith shop, a small tavern, and a single trader. The late Mr.
George Huntington informed me that in 1793, he arrived there
on horseback, and the tavern was unable to furnish him food for
his horse. He inquired if there was no one in the neighborhood
who could provide him with something to keep his animal from
starving. The answer was, there was no one but a farmer who
lived about half a mile westward who had hay and grain for his
own use, but none to spare and he would not sell it. He inquired
from where the farmer came, and was told from New England.
Mr. Huntington found a man to go to him with the horse and tell
the farmer that its owner was a young Yankee just arrived, and he
wished, on account of his Yankee brotherhood, that he would
entertain his starving horse. The farmer, who was the late
Stephen Potter, known both as Captain and Deacon Potter, was
pleased with the manner of the request and replied that he would
take care of the horse. The next day, when Mr. Huntington called
upon him, he refused to accept any pay for the service from his
Yankee brother. A lasting friendship was then commenced
between the two. I will here relate an anecdote of the Captain
and his friend, Mr. Huntington, which illustrates the integrity of
the Yankee farmer. Mr. Huntington had contracted for a large
tract of land on Frankfort Hill. The seller of the land had failed
to convey it and a suit was brought by Mr. Huntington for
damages, they depending upon the value of the land. It became
important to prove this and knowing that Captain Potter was
acquianted with the land, he directed his attorney to subpoena
him as a witness, but charged him not to offend the old gentleman by undertaking to get an opinion of him in advance as it
might lead him to suspect that it would be an attempt to induce
him on the strength of his friendship for Mr. Huntington to influence his testimony. The trial came on and the attorney refrained
from inquiring from Captain Potter in advance his opinion of the

value of the land. He called him to the witness stand. He asked him if he knew the land; he replied "Yes, every foot of it". "Well, Captain Potter, do you know its value?" "Yes, sir". "Very well, tell us what it is worth". The old gentleman paused a moment until the court, the jurors, and the spectators had fixed their eyes upon him when he slowly said, "Well, if I had all the gold that I could draw with my four yoke of oxen on a sled upon glare ice, and I had to invest every cent of it in land, I vow to God, I would not give a dollar an acre for it".

An involuntary shout of laughter filled the court house. Mr. Huntington at once discontinued the action, but his friendship with Captain Potter continued.

Until after the year 1800, no one foresaw the dimensions Utica was destined to attain in less than a century, nor dreamed that it would become the important commercial and manufacturing city it now is; the ornament of central New York with its abodes of wealth and cultivated taste, and adorned with its beautiful churches, educational establishments, and asylums for the relief of suffering infancy, and for the solace of those, who in the evening of their days, might suffer the evils of want and homeless poverty. The prophets of the day regarded the crossing place from the Mohawk to Wood Creek at Fort Stanwix, which connected the canoe navigation from Schenectady to Lake Ontario, as likely to become the site of the leading town in central New York. The length of this portage was but two miles. Enterprising men in the eastern part of the State, at a very early day, directed their attention to the connecting of the waters of the two streams so as to open a navigable channel for batteaux from Schenectady through Oneida Lake and the Oswego River to Lake Ontario. In March, 1792, an act was passed by the Legislature incorporating a company "for the purpose of opening a lock navigation from the navigable waters of the Hudson to Lakes Ontario and Seneca", under the style of "The Western Inland Lock Navigation Company." The company was organized with a board of directors consisting of some of the leading men in the State, with General Phillip Schuyler as president. An examination of the Mohawk, from Schenectady to its confluence with the Hudson, showed so many difficulties in its passage around the Cahoes, that it was deemed inexpedient to construct that part of the line. The company thereupon concluded to commence the navigation at Schenectady and by clearing out the shallow places on the Mohawk and Wood Creek and constructing a canal around the Little Falls

Rome Historical Society

Benjamin Wright (1770-1842)

and another from the Mohawk to Wood Creek, complete a navigation through Oneida Lake to Lake Ontario.

It is hardly credible at this day that there was not engineering skill in this country sufficient to direct the construction of this work; yet such was the fact. Mr. William Western, a gentleman of education and a skillful engineer, was brought from England to assume charge of the work at what was then deemed the enormous salary of £1,000 sterling per annum. The navigation was completed in 1797 and continued to be used until the Erie Canal was finished. The dimensions were too small to be very important as a channel of commerce. The locks were seventy feet in length and seven feet in width and calculated for the passage of batteaux drawing 21 inches of water. The boats navigating it could not, at the ordinary stage of water, carry more than five or six tons of cargo.

Another anecdote indicating the progress of engineering in this country may not be uninteresting. The late Benjamin Wright, of Rome, while a youth, spent some time with Baron Steuben, assisting him in the survey of his lands. While Mr. Western was engaged in superintending the construction of the canal and locks at Rome, Mr. Wright was employed by him as an assistant. After Mr. Western returned to England, General Schuyler expressed a regret to Mr. Huntington, who had charge of the canal, that he had not employed Mr. Western to make a topographical map of the Mohawk, as he knew no one who could be procured to do it. Mr. Huntington told him that he had a young man who could do it, and named Mr. Wright. General Schuyler employed him to make a survey and map showing the levels of the river and was delighted with the skill with which it was made.

When the law was passed for the construction of the Erie Canal, Mr. (then Judge) Wright was selected as one of the chief engineers and continued to discharge the duties of his office until it was finished. He was afterwards engaged in various important public works and was universally regarded in the very front rank of American engineers.

For several years Whitesboro continued to be the leading settlement and the commercial centre of the county. The road westward from Albany to Schenectady, then following up the north bank of the Mohawk, was still a country road, and a very poor one at that. In 1787, the first turnpike-road in the State was incorporated. It was to construct a turnpike between Albany and Schenectady. The company was not organized, and just a year after another act was passed incorporating a new company under the title of the Great Western Turnpike Company. This made the road from Albany westward.

It is to the construction of this turnpike-road that Utica is indebted for her subsequent growth. Commissioners were appointed to determine its route. It was a question with them where it should cross the Mohawk. The tradition is that Judge White was opposed to having roads with toll-gates. He wished all the roads to be free in his neighborhood so as to invite emigration; and he insisted to the commissioners that they should not cross at the old Sauquoit landing on this account. The late Jedediah Sangor had just established himself at New Hartford, and built a flour-mill there. He was a man of forethought, and foresaw the crossing at Fort Schuyler would necessitate a straight road to his settlement, and tend to built it up, and he had no fear of toll-gates. By his influence the road was made to cross there.

When the road was completed, Utica, instead of Rome or Whitesboro, became practically the head of the river navigation and the point of departure of wagon transportation for the western country. The navigation from Rome westward to Lake Ontario never became very important. Westward from Rome there was no good road to the line of the turnpike to furnish Rome a convenient point of departure from the river. The land lying westerly was a deep swamp. The turnpike engrossed the largest share of transportation from Utica westward, and a very considerable part of that from Albany. But up to 1804, Utica had not become so large a village as either Rome or Whitesboro.

The early settlers of Oneida County were, in a large proportion, men of intelligence, culture and enterprise. Within a very few years they erected churches and established schools in all the settlements. As early as 1793, Hamilton Oneida Academy, the germ of Hamilton College, was established. The Rev. Samuel Kirkland, the apostle of Christianity to the Heathen Oneidas, was the principal mover in the enterprise. This was the first incorporated academy west of Schenectady. Among its first trustees were General Alexander Hamilton, Chancellor Lansing, and Egbert Benson, then one of the justices of the Supreme Court. An academical building was erected, the corner-stone having been laid by Baron Steuben. The academy was originally intended to be enlarged into a college and, in 1812, a college charter was granted to it by the Board of Regents of the University. The charter was eminently a liberal one. It was intended that the college should be free from sectarianism. Its first board of trustees included leading farmers, clergymen, lawyers, and merchants, men of various denominations of religion. In 1823, when a committee of the trustees visited the college to make an examination in relation to a college difficulty, its members consisted of a Presbyterian, and Episcopalian, and a Roman Catholic.

As early as 1791, Congregational churches had been gathered in New Hartford, Kirkland and Marshall, through the missionary labors of Doctor Jonathan Edwards, familiarly known as the younger Edwards, who was subsequently president of Union College. In 1793, Presbyterian churches were founded in Whitesboro, Utica, Westmoreland and Trenton, and the next year in Camden and Augusta. In most of the other towns, churches of various denominations had been organized. An Episcopal church was gathered in Utica in 1798, by the Rev. Philander Chase, afterwards, Bishop of Ohio and Illinois, and within a short time, another in Paris.

The origin of the Baptist church in Oneida County is interesting as showing the character of one of its principal founders and his influence in building up his denomination there.

In 1796, Rev. Stephen Parsons organized a Baptist church in Whitesboro and received to its communion, Caleb Douglass, then a blacksmith. Mr. Parsons remained its pastor but a few years, when Mr. Douglass, who had been the most active of its members, was called to the ministry as its pastor. This was in 1802. He was a man of great energy and of profound religious convictions. As a part of his belief, the Christian minister should not pass a definite stage of preparation for his work, but should, by careful reading of the holy scriptures and prayer, qualify himself so, that led by the immediate influences of the Holy Spirit, he could faithfully and effectively preach the gospel. As a necessary consequence, the Christian pastor should not be paid for his services. He should not, in the language of the day, be a hireling. These two positions he earnestly inculcated in his preachings and pastoral visitations. And he illustrated them by his practice. He continued to be a blacksmith on week days working at his anvil, and on Sundays, administering to the spiritual wants of his flock; and instead of being indebted to his congregation for any part of his support, his house was the abode of hospitality for his brethren and the sojourn of his parishioners during the interval of worship on Sunday. He continued to preach to his people and to perform missionary labor in gathering and organizing Baptist churches and administering the sacraments throughout the county and in the neighboring towns for some twelve or fifteen years. He frequently urged upon his hearers the evils of a learned and a hireling clergy. At length, a young man who had been graduated at Dartmouth College and had been ordained in the Baptist church, visited Elder Douglass. He was induced by him to remain his guest until the next Sunday when he preached for him in both morning and afternoon services. It was Elijah W. Willey, subsequently an approved and successful Baptist minister for many years. When Mr. Willey closed his afternoon service, Elder Douglass arose, and addressing his congregation, told them that he had administered to them in sacred things some fifteen years and had endeavored to lay before them the bread of life to the best of his ability; that they knew his views concerning the sacred ministry; that he had often warned them against a learned and a hireling ministry; that his views had yielded to his deep convictions of his error; that he had experienced the want of more learning to render his preaching properly instructive; that he was now convinced that a pastor should be well educated in Christian learning and that he should be constantly acquiring knowledge to be the pastor as well as the teacher of his flock; to do this he must have leisure and must be supported by his church, and become, what he had frequently designated, a hireling. He then told that he had become an old man and soon must give up his labors, when his church would have to receive another to become their Christian pastor. They had now present a young brother, who had the advantages of education, who had just preached to them. He would be happy if they would chose him to be their minister and pay him for his services, a salary sufficient to support him. To show them that he was in earnest, he proposed they should start a subscription for the purpose, and he would lead it with what was a large sum.

The good old man resumed his seat. The congregation was astounded, but they had unlimited confidence in the judgment of the elder, and his argument had commanded universal assent. The subscription was filled and Elder Willey was installed as a learned and hireling pastor. The good old blacksmith, after a few years, removed from Whitesboro to a western town where he subsequently died in a good old age, universally respected and beloved. It is many years since, but those of his acquaintances who survive, remember him with affection and cherish his memory as of a saintly man more worthy of honor and respect as an apostle of his faith than thousands who are decorated with the degrees of half a dozen universities. It is now rare to find Baptists who do not regard education and pastoral support with favor, and its members are generally inclined to award a generous support to their ministers.

A notice of the erection of the first Methodist church in Rome will awaken the memories of some of the older of my auditors. A Methodist society was formed in that village early in the present century, but until 1826, it had no place of worship. Its members had become prosperous in their circumstances and concluded to erect a church. They very naturally wished to erect one to compare in architectural beauty favorably with those of the other religious communities in the town. After due consideration, the trustees adopted a plan for one with a modest steeple in two sections. A Methodist meeting house with a steeple was then unusual, and the consciences of a portion of the brethren and sisters who adhered rigidly to the early traditions of Methodism, were not a little disturbed as such a manifest departure from Christian simplicity. Church meetings were called and sharp lines drawn between the steeple and no-steeple men and women, and abundance of theological logic was brought into play. The question was brought before the lowest church court and then carried by successive appeals to the highest - the general conference then held at Pittsburgh. After profound and learned arguments, this body disposed of the question to the satisfaction of most of the two parties by adjudging that as the lowest section of the steeple would serve a good purpose for a belfry and hold a bell to call people to church - that might stand, but that the upper section not being intended for use but merely for ornament, like other vanities, should be abandoned by sober Christian people.

The judgment was submitted to and carried out, and it was said that this was the first Meeting House in the land with a steeple. Some, however, of the older members of the church, used to their day of the death, to call it a "steeple house".

The Methodists, since then, have made decided progress in Church architecture. At this day, some of the handsomest ecclesiastical structures in the country have been built by Churches of their denomination.

The march of Oneida County, during the whole period of its history, has been largely owing to the high standing of her early inhabitants in intelligence and culture. A large proportion of its men and women were persons of superior intelligence and worth in their several positions. The political questions that agitated the whole American people, were held with singular tenacity. Under the first four Presidents of the United States, there was a decided predominance of Federalists in the country. Until the days of Jacksonism, the method of nominations to public office by both parties was not made, as now, by delegated conventions and primary meetings. An invitation would be published inviting the members of the party to a county meeting to make nomination of candidates. These meetings were generally attended by but few gentlemen. Those present selected candidates, whom they recommended. I remember, in my boyish days, going to see what turned out to be the last Federalist meeting held in the County. It was called to nominate candidates for election to the Assembly, the old courthouse in Whitesboro being the place of meeting, and not being half filled. After the meeting was organized, a committee was formed to recommend persons for candidates. They reported a ticket with the late General Joseph Kirkland at its head. He arose and, thanking his friends for the compliment, respectfully declined the honor. A vote was about being taken on a motion to excuse him. He again arose and declared that his engagements would not permit him to accept the nomination and asked that some one might be selected to fill the place. The meeting laughed at his remonstrance, voted unanimously not to excuse him, and insisted that he must be the candidate.

I was present some years after this at a meeting of those who favored the second election of John Quincy Adams to the presidency. It was held at the Presbyterian Church in Whitesboro, which was crowded, as it was understood that the late Henry R. Storrs, who was then a member of Congress, would address his constituents. This was simply a county meeting. After an eloquent address by Mr. Storrs, an elector was nominated with entire unanimity.

The first nomination of Mr. Storrs to Congress illustrates the habits of the politicians of the day. Since 1820, Oneida County has, with singular unanimity, adhered to, what in the days of Henry Clay, was called the American system - favoring a protective tariff. But it was not always so.

Prior to the war of 1812, cotton and woolen factories had been erected in several towns, and the wants of the country during the war had given to them prosperity. After the war, Congress revised its tariff in the interest of protection. This did not meet the views of some of the farmers, who were staunch federalists. In 1820, there was a congressman to be elected, and the leading men of the Federal party were in favor of selecting the late James Lynch, afterwards of New York, then a resident of Rome. He was a gentleman of high social position, good standing at the bar, and of pleasing manners. He had lived at Rome several years where he had built a large mill and satinet factory. No one else was spoken of as the person to be nominated. The county meeting assembled. It was composed of a few leading men from Whitesboro and Utica and a few of the most influential farmers of the vicinity. A committee was constituted of five or six members to select and report to the meeting, a candidate. The Chairman of the meeting named the committee, placing upon it three of the farmers, who were leading men in their towns. The committee retired to consult, and the farmers happened to be opposed in principle to a protective tariff, and afraid to send anyone to Congress who owned a satinet factory, and who would, of course, as they supposed be, in favor of legislative protection to manufacturers. The other members of the committee tried to quiet their opposition, but in those days, nominations were regarded as simple recommendations and were not made by bargain and sale to be carried by the force of political machinery, which first buys up a convention and then registers its decrees to be carried out by dragooning the simple members of the party, under whip and spur, to sustain them. After earnest discussion, it was found impossible to overcome the free trade scruples of the farmers on the committee, when a gentleman proposed the name of the late Henry R. Storrs. This was satisfactory to all and he was reported to the meeting as the candidate and adopted by the meeting by a unanimous vote. He was subsequently elected. This was the commencement of his political career. Judge Bacon, in his lecture on the bar of Oneida County, has given you a happy sketch of him. He possessed talents as an orator at the bar and in Congress, that have never been excelled. He had a commanding person, with a wonderfully rich and flexible voice. In the open air, he could speak in a whisper so as to be heard by an audience of ten thousand men; and he could elevate it to thunder tones without stretching it. His gesticulations were exceedingly graceful. He possessed a rare command of language and his mind was filled with elegant learning always at his command. His power over his audience was electric, whether exercised, to excite merriment or tears, or to carry conviction to the reason. Henry Clay said of him that he was the most eloquent man who had ever spoken in Congress.

During Mr. Storrs' first congressional term, the Country was agitated with the question of admitting Missouri without the power to hold slaves. Mr. Storrs was of opinion that Congress had no power under the terms of the compact by which her territory had been acquired and the laws passed inviting its original inhabitants to bring their slaves into the territory to impose the condition upon her. He therefore voted for her admission without restriction. It was an unfortunate vote and he was so censured for it by his friends that he declined a re-election and General Kirkland was called to his place. At the end of the term of the latter, Mr. Storrs was nominated for the position by the "Bucktail Party", as it was called, formed from democrats opposed to DeWitt Clinton, and oldtime federalists, whose early warfare against Mr. Clinton led them instinctively to oppose him. Mr. Storrs was elected and, at the next election, became a candidate in opposition to the Democratic party and was re-elected. He was twice after this elected, and it had become understood that it mattered little who nominated or opposed him, he would command the vote of Oneida County. At the close of his fifth term, he removed to the City of New York where he practiced his profession during the residue of his life.

I may, here to, advert to a controversy which once excited Utica and the towns of Whitestown and Rome, but which has long since been forgotten by most of your citizens. Whitesboro and Rome had, at an early day, been the seats of courthouses and divided the courts of record. By the year 1817, Utica had grown beyond the limits of both these villages, and its inhabitants conceived the idea of making it the single shire town of the county. It was perfectly clear to the Uticans that it was the central town and the proper place for the courts. The early supremacy of Rome and Whitestown was held for naught, very much to the disgust of their inhabitants who had borne the front in the battle of pioneerism and who boasted the possession of the most learned lawyers in the county. They were aroused and sent agents throughout the northern towns obtaining remonstrances against the proposed wrong, and by placards posted in every tavern and horse-shed, depicted the disasters that would flow over the county, and indeed the State, from the removal of the courts. Among other things to protect themselves and the County, a newspaper was established in Rome under the name of the Oneida Observer, which continued there until the courthouse controversy was terminated by the triumph of the joint power of Rome and Whites-

Barber & Howe Historical Collections

Southwest view of Oneida Institute, Whitestown, one of the first bi-racial schools in the country.

boro, when the newspaper was transferred to the democratic party and removed to Utica. I believe the journal is perpetuated under the same name and that it has, during its whole existence, done battle valiantly for the democratic party in all its windings and turnings of doctrine.

Whitesboro, for many years, continued to hold half the county courts, and, divided with Rome, one half the circuit courts; until at length, Utica quietly absorbed them all. With this exception, I believe that Oneida County has never had a general quarrel among its citizens. A little generous rivalry was awakened at the time the Black River Railroad was projected, but the strife soon ceased when the rival parties had come to the bottom of their purses. The ancient friendship was then speedily restored and Rome entered upon a new course of progress which has made it one of the most beautiful cities in the State.

The labors of the early inhabitants of Oneida County achieved for it a high standing among the counties of the State. No one of them has enjoyed the labors of a more learned and self-devoted clergy; none has had a more talented and accomplished bar; none a more distinguished body of medical practitioners; no county has distinguished itself more in institutions for the relief of suffering and infirmity; few counties but Oneida have had their large hearted Faxtons with the spirit of Peter Cooper, to become the executors of their own wills in bestowing the fruits of long life labors for the cause of education and humanity. Your orphan asylums and homes for the aged and infirm, your public schools and academies; and your Hamilton College and your Whitesboro Seminary have been producing the legitimate results of their creation; and among other associations, your society formed to perpetuate the story of its progress. Nowhere are more beautiful farms, more tasteful homesteads with their ornamental grounds and gardens to be found, and he who can ride throughout your territory without admiration of its landscapes must be singularly unappreciative of real beauty.

The first white settler of Oneida was Samuel Kirkland, her apostle - a missionary of the cross. Many of the sons of Oneida have followed his example by giving their lives as Christian missionaries to heathen lands all over the globe. I should love to rehearse to you all their names, but most of them are graven on your memories and will be known and remembered wherever the records of Christian missions shall be preserved. Of the sons of her early settlers, two have been Senators in Congress and three or four members of the House of Representatives, and among them an Admiral and two Commodores in the Navy, and several Generals in the Army.

Index